DAWN OF A NEW DAY:

My Journey to Nonprofit Success

BY DAWN L. MURRAY

Publisher's Note:

Spirit Led Publishing and Printing Group
Atlanta, Georgia

ISBN - 978-1-7329054-3-6

ISBN 978-1-7329054-3-6

9 781732 905436 >

Cover design, internal formatting & layout: Hemant Lal
www.AaronProductionsIndia.com

DEDICATION: TO DADDY

As I was trying to start House of Dawn you gave me so many words of wisdom and scriptures to help keep me focused on this ministry. You told me it wouldn't be easy, but to keep pushing and always give God the glory.

Thank you, Daddy, for your strength, encouragement, and for believing in me.

You embodied so many unforgettable traits such as your contagious smile, your magnetic personality, and love for family. I share these traits with every young mother and child who encounter House of Dawn.

As you look down from heaven, I hope that you are proud of your little girl!

Why reinvent the wheel? Dawn has already done the work as this book gives readers the tools to live their dreams. This easy read walks us through her journey as Ms. Murray learns what works and what doesn't. Dawn of a New Day prepares you for the inevitable roadblocks that lie ahead so that you recognize when to proceed with caution while traveling your own journey to success.

Sheila Taylor, Founder, Ollies Place Specialty Suites, Inc.

The House of Dawn programs are a prime example of Dawn's passion for people and her caring heart. Her journey has been long and tedious at times, but there have also been many celebrations and victories along the way! Like its author, this book will be a blessing to so many.

Dr. Felicia Barnett

Most CEOs can speak to the high-level goals and theoretical ideas their organization is espousing. For House of Dawn, the approach is real-life coping skills, high expectations of clients, and a mix of love and praise that uplifts the human spirit. We have witnessed through House of Dawn's work under Ms. Murray that by elevating each mother and child, they are affecting a positive outcome for future generations.

Joy B. Day, M.S. Ed.S.
Mayor, City of Jonesboro, Georgia

CONTENTS

FOREWORD

I begin this foreword to Dawn of a New Day: My Journey to Nonprofit Success by defining the word serendipity, which means "the occurrence and development of events by chance in a happy or beneficial way." This word is significant because it best describes how I view and began my relationship with the author of this book, Dawn Leneice Murray.

There are other words that could also describe my relationship with Dawn, such as accident, fluke, fortuitous, providence, coincidence, and/or kismet. Whichever word intrigues you most, know that the opportunity to participate in the birth, growth, and development of House of Dawn, Inc. has been one of the highlights of my life both professionally and spiritually.

After being asked to write the foreword to this eagerly awaited "must read" detailing Dawn's vision, motivation, and subsequent journey to the realization of what is now the House of Dawn, I began to reflect on how I became a part of this story.

Just as Dawn was given the vision, I was given a gift: to have a hand in the initial planning and development of House of Dawn. As events unfolded over a protracted period of time and after much labor, numerous trials, and challenges, House of Dawn became a reality.

So, why was I selected to work with Dawn on this mission? It is said that the journey of a lifetime begins with a single step. In our case, it began with a telephone call seeking information and guidance. This space does not permit me to share all of the captivating, intricate, personal, and at times, irritating details about how House of Dawn was born, but I will share some context.

At the time I worked for another agency that provided housing and an array of intensive social services which offered parenting assistance to teen girls and their children. One day the telephone rang and on the other end was Dawn Murray asking to speak with the agency's program director.

Dawn proceeded to explain her desire to open a group home for parenting teens and their children. She mentioned being rebuffed by others who told her to "struggle like they had" when asked to share information about how to make this happen. Annoyed upon hearing this I not only agreed to speak with Dawn, but to do so in person.

Allow me to help you visualize the very tall, well-dressed, strikingly attractive young woman who walked into my office that day. Yes, Ms. Murray presented well. Her demeanor was all at once friendly, serious, compelling, and extremely thoughtful. I could tell that she was not going to be deterred, as she arrived seeking solutions while refusing to accept defeat.

After touring the group home and my office, we talked a lot about Dawn's vision for the program itself. I shared the philosophy that guides the work required to help parenting teens and their children, such as the rules and regulations of operating under the auspices of The Georgia Division of Family and Children Services (DFCS) which places both mother and child into the home, and the Office of Regulatory Services which licenses all group homes. We also talked about who her community sponsors and supporters were, because nobody can do this work in a vacuum.

I was impressed with Dawn's eagerness to learn as I listened to her enthusiasm for opening a group home. We both knew that her vision to serve parenting teens who wanted to keep their children instead of putting them up for adoption or placing them in the protection of the DFCS could fill a vital gap in her county, which struggled with a high teen pregnancy rate.

Dawn also shared details about her personal life, including her beautiful and supportive family who I came to love. They partly fueled her resolve to deliver continued education, training, and housing to parenting teens.

Our meeting is what led to my six-year stint as House of Dawn's first Executive Program Director, a herculean role that included program manager responsibilities for directing the nonprofit's day-to-day operations, the managing and training of personnel, client base case management, and a myriad of other tasks too numerous to list here. While these tasks were daunting at times, I was blessed to witness this organization's tremendous growth and commitment to serving parenting teens and children desperately in need of safety, love, care, education, and training. Being a part of House of Dawn's story is an honor that I do not take lightly and is greatly appreciated.

But Dawn's journey to nonprofit success expanded beyond simply establishing housing for parenting teens and their children. The reduction of teen pregnancy and parenting education eventually produced a "for-profit" arm designed to help others interested in establishing their own 501(c)(3) nonprofit agencies. Her workshops also promote self-esteem through training and best practices in entrepreneurship and women's empowerment.

I am so proud of the amazing work that Dawn – along with her staff and supporters – have done and will continue to do. The young women who have successfully passed through House of Dawn's programs are the manifestation of every positive value that has been instilled in them. What a blessed cause for thanksgiving – and there are more blessings to come!

Only God knows the outcome of every human being. Our job as directors, counselors, teachers, mentors, parents, and funders is to plant the seeds, provide the resources and opportunities, and nurture with love, discipline, information, and guidance. Under Dawn's guidance, House of Dawn continues to do that.

Finally, to Dawn: may your book be the success that I know it will be, and may you continue to enjoy the fruits of your labor. Continue to grow professionally and may God ever continue to bless you to be a blessing to others.

Yvonne Veanice Prioleau, *MSS, LMSW*
Former Executive Program Director, House of Dawn, Inc.
2005-2011

PREFACE

This House of Dawn journey grew into an unbelievable faith walk for me. The more hurdles we jumped over, the deeper my faith in the Lord became. My Daddy told me when we opened House of Dawn that it should be done in such a way that only He could get the Glory! Daddy was right.

Did I feel like giving up at times? Absolutely. But I didn't. I surrounded myself with positive people who have supported and encouraged me in this work. This makes me truly blessed, providing me with the means to pass those blessings on to others.

So . . . why did I write this book? Because I want my struggles to prevent your struggles.

My goal is to inspire people to step out on faith and live their passion. No matter how hard it seems or how many roadblocks you face, do not give up!

As you move through this book you will read about the highs and lows, the battles and the accolades. I have also provided tools to help with your own start-up, such as checklists and Nonprofit Nuggets. These tools are useful whether your organization identifies as a nonprofit or for-profit.

So, turn the pages, follow the script, and be the success that you planned to be!

Acknowledgements

Mr. Mumford

Layne

Mrs. Smith

Chapter 1

MY ORIGIN STORY

"I was born to do this – this is my purpose!"

It was a crisp fall day in November and the golden amber leaves were already falling off of the trees. I remember because my mom had started pulling the plastic containers that housed our sweaters and other winter clothing from under the bed.

Thanksgiving was fast approaching when my third-grade teacher, Mrs. Morgan, explained that the class needed to collect canned goods for the homeless and families in need. I knew we weren't the richest family on the block, but the way my teacher spoke about the needy made me empathetic. So much so that I excitedly carried canned goods to school for two days straight.

My father, who worked security at night, came home early one morning before I left for school. He went looking in the pantry for a can of corn beef hash and noticed it was emptier than usual.

"What happened, Baby? Didn't we have enough money for food this month?" he called out with a mix of alarm and agitation. "Where is all the food?"

"There's food in there!" my mother replied defensively, as she came to help search the pantry. That's when my siblings and I got called into the kitchen for questioning – specifically about where that corn beef hash went.

"Oh, I took it to school to give to the needy for Thanksgiving," I said nonchalantly. When I took those cans, it never occurred to ask either of my parents if it was okay to do so. I just felt compelled to help.

In that moment, the look on both my parents face was straight out of a Good Times episode as they channeled James and Florida Evans. My father then gently put his arms around my shoulders and whispered, "You know what Dawnie? We are the needy!" he said while laughing out loud, making the rest of us laugh.

The truth is, I always enjoyed helping people and believe that I was put on this earth to nurture others. Whether in school or at home, I was always the kid that others came to with their problems. My parents were like second parents to our friends, which meant we often had a houseful of kids enjoying food, fun, and laughter. The door was open to all, whether they were in need or not.

This is my origin story. And while I didn't realize it back then, I was a little social worker in the making.

Chapter 2

THE DECEPTIVE STRUGGLE
OF CORPORATE AMERICA

"I hated my job!"

I was given a vision in my early twenties of working with teenage mothers and their children to provide them with housing and supportive services.

But I didn't have any money. I had no idea how to start a business. In fact, I knew no one who had ever started such a business, and certainly didn't know the differences between a for-profit business versus a nonprofit.

So, I started from the beginning and along the way struggled to find out information because some people were unwilling to share.

In the meantime, I worked in corporate America. I had great benefits, enjoyed what I was doing, liked my co-workers, and was learning a lot. As I watched many of my friends search for a career path, I was actually on the right track and even looking forward to climbing the corporate ladder.

I excelled at my position, which encouraged my supervisors and managers to give me even more work. But I was glad to see that they trusted me and hoped it would eventually lead to higher pay and promotions.

Adding insult to injury, I ended up training people who were getting paid more and promoted faster. Of course, the silver-tongued senior management offered all the right words, compliments, and promises as they asked me to train, mentor, and monitor incoming employees. I humbly accepted but had immediate concerns about one particular trainee who obviously knew nor cared anything about the job. The trainee was there to collect a check and seemingly planned on doing only mediocre work. But here I was feeling ownership and loyalty to this company that forced me to train someone who had a different agenda.

Raise your hand if this has happened to you. Slap your own hand if you are that employee.

Needless to say, I took the trainee under my wing. I believe that my dedication rubbed off on this person, who eventually became engaged in the mission and vison of this company and went on to get promoted as well.

Getting that person onto the right career path still didn't solve my problem, however.

Despite being used to training some of this company's best employees, my commitment and hard work were not reciprocated. I went to my supervisor and asked if all this additional work would eventually come with an increase in pay or a promotion. I never got a straight answer despite continually being told, "You're doing a great job! Just add it to your resume as experience."

As a married woman with two young children at the time – a three-year-old and a four-month-old – all I could think was how ideal it would be if I could get a job working from home. These types of positions were becoming pretty popular with businesses and seemed beneficial for both the employer and employee. Everything about my job, including all the new tasks that I was doing, could actually be done from home.

I approached my manager about starting a work from home program, and thankfully he seemed interested. He told me to design the program and bring the plan back to him.

In the meantime, my schedule at that time was not enviable. After working my corporate job from 8:00 a.m. to 5:00 p.m. I'd fight Atlanta traffic to get to the day care by 6:00 p.m. At home I'd cook dinner while entertaining and spending quality time with my babies. Then I would bathe and put them to bed, and start preparations for the next day.

I would then stay up late to perfect my job's work from home program while waiting for my then-husband, Jerome, to get home from work. I would only get a few hours of sleep because I had to get up by 5:30 a.m. and start the day all over again. But I needed to give this project my all because my work-life balance depended on it!

I poured my heart and soul into designing the program, taking the needs of all parties into consideration. I thought for sure this would be my payoff for all of the hard work, dedication, and loyalty I had shown the company thus far. Working from home could make up for the lack of raises and promotions I'd missed out on thus far.

After developing the program and making sure all bases were covered, I presented it to my manager. He was very impressed and had me to present the proposal to upper management.

I was extremely nervous, but ready to sell the company on my plan. I had to leave the same heart and soul I had poured into developing the program on the boardroom table. Everything was at stake.

The room was quiet as I was introduced, and began to speak. Their facial expressions were as still and serious as those chiseled into Mount Rushmore. This is my chance I thought to myself – I had to remove my fears and go for it. I spoke professionally and passionately as I watched their chiseled expressions slowly begin to soften. After completing the presentation, I was assured they would get back with me soon.

About six months later, it was announced that the company's accounting department was offering a new work from home program. But I was not offered one of the positions in this new program.

I was furious to say the least. They didn't even give me the courtesy of an explanation after I patiently waited for a response. What really hurt was that other employees were about to benefit from all of my hard work.

At least boost my ego, say thank you but you are too valuable to be outside of the office right now. Compromise and allow me to work from home for a few days each week. Instead, they said nothing until the announcement was made to the entire company as if they had developed this program on their own. What moral compass were these people conducting business with?

I had given birth to a corporate incentive that was stolen from me. I went from loving my job to despising it.

Chapter 3

MY LIFE-CHANGING DOCTOR VISIT

"Every Superwoman has her breaking point."

Despite my disappointment, I still went to work every day, but it just wasn't the same.

I felt used, unappreciated, and my morale was virtually nonexistent. The hurt and anger made me so resentful that every time I pulled into the company parking lot, I instantly got a migraine. This toxic environment was now literally making me sick.

One day, I was supposed to host a colleague's baby shower after work in the breakroom when suddenly my body just felt strange. Although I was experiencing a horrible headache in the back of my head, this was different from the parking lot migraines.

While walking under the breezeway approaching my office building, an especially cold wind blew. That's when I felt an earache on the same side of my head as the headache, which continued all day. I went into the mailroom across from my cubicle and asked a co-worker three times throughout the day if my smile looked crooked because my face felt off-kilter. Each time she told me no.

The final time I asked, she laughed. "Girl, would you go on! I told you, there is nothing wrong with your face or your smile!" she responded through laughter. Each ask was followed by a trip to the ladies room to look in the mirror for myself. The weird feeling intensified as the day progressed, but my appearance never seemed to change. I began to wonder if this was all just in my head. My colleague enjoyed her baby shower and I was able to stay upbeat through the entire thing.

Earlier that day my mother-in-law picked the kids up from day care, which she often did when work got in the way. Once we got home I managed to complete our usual routine, but while feeding and giving them baths I was still feeling that horrible pain in the back of my head.

That's when I called my mom, telling her how I'd been feeling all day. I already decided to go to the doctor once Jerome got home but my mother insisted I go immediately, warning that the symptoms sounded like I might be having a stroke.

I felt like Mom was overreacting and still headed to the doctor after he got home. I knew something was very wrong, but as a twenty-four-year-old woman in relatively good health, surely, I couldn't be having a stroke!

By the time I sat down in the waiting room my facial sensations felt different – not like earlier at work when it felt a little numb and crooked, but as if it were actually twisting. By the time I got in front of the doctor my face quickly became completely twisted, my eye would not close, and the left side of my face was completely paralyzed. The medical team ruled out a stroke, but I was diagnosed with Bell's Palsy – something I had never even heard of before.

My life changed in an instant. I was given a prescription of steroids and an eye ointment. I had to sleep with this ointment in my eye and a patch over it to keep it from drying out because I couldn't close it. My speech was slurred and my words were hard to understand.

Most people would have stayed home from work after receiving news like this and feeling the way I did. But not me. I got up the next day and continued my regimen of hard work and dedication. My colleagues were in disbelief at how much my appearance and speech pattern changed literally overnight. My speech was so slurred that I couldn't even talk on the phone. "You kept saying you felt funny yesterday, I'm so sorry," said the co-worker that I had been harassing the day before about my appearance.

It was only when I tried to eat breakfast at my desk that I realized I couldn't eat or drink without everything falling out of my mouth. It was my co-workers who helped me learn how to eat and drink again. One noticed if I moved food to the side of my mouth that wasn't paralyzed, I could at least chew on that side without the food falling out of my mouth. Seeing how liquid would run out of my mouth we practiced drinking with a straw the same way, which also worked. I eventually got used to eating and drinking on the right side of my mouth in order to hold everything in.

Overall, my colleagues were wonderful and helped me adapt to my new normal. I couldn't believe just how quickly my life was so negatively impacted.

But it all made sense to the doctors as I described the length of my days and strenuous routines. They confirmed that my condition was brought on by stress and in that moment, I realized that my need to be Superwoman had taken its toll. I was so busy juggling and taking care of everyone else that I neglected my own health. It was unbelievable that putting my needs last seemed to have left me paralyzed.

In addition, my list of personal and professional responsibilities had begun to weigh me down so much, that my physical and emotional health were now at risk.

Bottom line – I was stressing over a job that I could no longer tolerate.

Oftentimes women are working full-time, caring for husbands, significant others, children, and aging parents while cooking, cleaning, washing clothes, and anything else they can fit in between those tasks. Knowing women die at a higher rate than men of stroke and heart disease, I'm blessed to have not suffered a stroke.

Nonprofit Nugget: *Self-care is important and stress is real!*

I thought I could be Superwoman – more importantly, I wanted to be. I thought repeatedly about the "should have, could have, would have" choices, but it was too late to change the past, I now had to move forward. I had to make some changes in my life and realize that I'm not a Superwoman. And admit to myself that this is okay.

Chapter 4

MY CONVERSATION WITH GOD

"What steps should I take?"

One morning a co-worker noticed that my Bell's Palsy seemed to look a little worse. I was clearly stressed, so she took me into the bathroom where we prayed together. She recited and shared scripture, advising me to read it often as a reminder of God's word.

After prayer, meditation, and writing in my journal, I felt He was telling me to start my own business. Doing so would eliminate at least some of the obstacles I faced while working at a thankless job. It would also provide the flexibility my family needed and most importantly, I'd be doing work that I actually enjoyed.

However, I still wasn't sure exactly what I wanted to do or how. What type of business should I venture into? How do I start it? Where would the money come from? These were questions off the top of my head, with so many more to follow.

Then one day God spoke to me. But at the time I was unsure of what the voice I was hearing was trying to telling me.

Despite the uncertainty, I had already learned program development, accounting, training, balancing general ledgers, and team leadership at work, among other things. Best of all, I got to see and practice the best way to implement these skills for my new business.

He illuminated that these were the very things that I needed to know. At that moment, I realized that God had been telling me to start my own business and preparing me to do so throughout my corporate journey!

*   *   *

Every day on my drive home from work I'd pass the Treetop Learning Academy. But as I passed the building for the umpteenth time, I felt a burning in the pit of my stomach. I always had a love for children and even enjoyed running a small in-home day care after my son was born. But this stirring made me wonder . . . *was this the business I should pursue?* The concept stayed on my heart and one day I pulled into the parking lot to pray, asking God if He was telling me to open a day care.

The next day I called Treetop to ask if the owner would be willing to speak with me about what it took to open a day care center, and was able to get an appointment a few days later. I still wasn't sure if this was the path I should follow, but needed to investigate further.

I arrived anxious to speak with the owner, who advised that she'd be with me as soon as possible. Happy for the opportunity to connect, I said no problem. After passing me by three or four more times she stopped to apologize, stating she just got a case that was taking her much longer than she anticipated to resolve.

On this extremely cold winter morning, a kid came into the day care announcing that he, his brothers, and mom had been sleeping in their van. The owner was calling around trying to get this family into a shelter, but they all were full. "We have day cares on every corner in this neighborhood. What we need are some more shelters around here!" she said out of frustration. Seeing that she was busy, we agreed to reschedule our meeting so that she could focus on helping that family.

But something about the day care owner's comment shook me, and I once again felt a burning in the pit of my stomach. I began to pray and ask God if he meant for me to open a shelter, because I couldn't get that idea out of my mind.

Another building that I had been passing for years was located in Hapeville, Georgia. I knew this was a homeless shelter, which had the day care owner's words echoing in my head. So, I began researching what it would take to start and operate a shelter to see if this was something that I wanted to do. After finding the organization's name, I again called to set up an appointment to learn more, just as I had done with Treetop.

The Hope Shelter's owner, Mr. Mumford, agreed to give me a tour and then patiently and kindly walked me step-by-step through what I needed to do to open a shelter. I took notes that day, but started visiting pretty often and volunteering in order to learn about all of the shelter's moving parts. The owner, who had now become my mentor, would tell me more about what I needed to do to start my own shelter.

With every visit I learned something new, continued taking notes, and gathered information for my "to do" list. I figured out what tasks to accomplish and how by the time my mentor and I met again. I was careful not to waste his time, and he was very impressed when I was able to show him the results of my efforts.

And although I was sure that God was telling me to start a shelter, I still wasn't sure what type of shelter or who I wanted to help. So, I then started praying to God asking him who He wanted me to help, and who He wanted me to serve. As I waited on the answer, I continued to volunteer at the shelter, meet with my mentor, and learn as much as I could.

While volunteering, a teenage girl whose parents had put her out because she was pregnant (she was actually pregnant with twins) arrived looking for shelter. Unfortunately, she had to be turned away, which confused me because she was obviously in need and this was a homeless shelter.

"Underage pregnant girls come here often, but I have to turn them away because I can't take teenagers. It's against state regulations for my shelter, and there's nowhere in Clayton County to send homeless teenage mothers," Mr. Mumford explained.

I instantly felt like a fire was lit in my stomach. In that moment, I knew I would open a shelter for homeless pregnant and parenting teenage mothers. I went home that night and thanked God for answering my prayers by revealing who I was to serve.

Throughout this process I learned a lot. At the age of twenty-four, I was truly learning to hear from God, learning to wait on Him, and had truly begun a walk of faith. Realizing I didn't know how I was going to do any of this, I knew it was what He was telling me to do and I asked in faith for Him to tell me how to do it and put the right people in my path to help me.

Chapter 5

THE VISION

"I was now pregnant with this vision and I couldn't be more excited!"

This vision – or rather, this ministry – was now crystal clear. So much so that not only could I see it, I could feel its weight in the pit of my stomach. I was excited about getting the opportunity to help young mothers – and I just couldn't hide it.

I also recognized how personally connected I was to its outcome. While I was never a teen mother myself, I was the product of a teen mother.

You see, my mother was married and had her first child, my sister, at the age of seventeen. In those days, people married early, but she was technically still a teen mother. By age twenty-one, Mom was divorced and left to care for three young children. She eventually met my father, and I was born five years later.

As I recall the stories of her struggles, she never let being a teen mother stop her from becoming successful or doing anything that she really wanted to do. She pushed through and made something of herself, setting the example that I went on to share with the young women who passed through House of Dawn.

She also shared with me that her sister, cousins, and even brothers were all teen parents. I remember throughout my childhood she would often say, "The generational curse of teen parenting stops with this generation. My girls will not be teen parents." It did stop and we were not teen mothers.

Reflecting on my upbringing was the confirmation that yes, I should open a home for teenage mothers.

I knew that I wanted it to look and feel like a warm, loving home – not a shelter. I wanted it to be the home that some of these young women had never had. I wanted to make sure that they finished school – even if they had dropped out at one point, this was their chance to go back.

We would have an onsite day care for the babies while the moms attended school during the day. I wanted to teach them both life and parenting skills so that they could parent their own kids and not be dependent on the program or anyone else. I wanted to give them the tools to make them independent, self-supporting women who were loving mothers to their children just like my mother was.

Life does not end with teen pregnancy for the mother nor the children. We would provide them with all the opportunities and second chances that we could.

Excited, I could not wait to get to work the next day and tell my co-workers that I now knew what God wanted me to do. I was going to open a home for teenage mothers and their children. They too were excited as we began to talk about it daily. That same young lady who prayed with me in the bathroom at work would often pray with me about this new assignment.

Chapter 6

STARTING A NONPROFIT

"Having a vision or even a directive from the Lord is one thing. Having the determination to grow that vision into reality requires faith, persistence, and a lot of hard work."

Armed with my notes and the knowledge learned from my mentor, I went right to work.

One of the first things I needed to do was become a nonprofit organization. I was not even sure what that was at the time, so I researched and continued thinking about what I needed to do.

But I still needed a name for my organization, so I began researching how to choose a business name and reserve it.

I shared with co-workers how much I loved the Serenity Prayer, which I really wanted to use in the business name. But as I checked to see what was available, every name I liked that included the word "serenity" was already taken.

As we brainstormed potential names one of my co-workers asked, "Leneice, what do you think about the name House of Dawn? It would signify a new start and a new beginning for the young moms who will be staying at the house."

The irony was that everyone only knew me by my middle name, Leneice, which I started using when I moved to Georgia. Neither of the co-workers I had this conversation with ever knew my first name. Yet the name was perfect for my organization. When I told her all of this, we both broke out in laughter.

Checklist 1: Reserving Your Business Name.

I ran to my computer to check if the name was available with the Secretary of State's office, and it was! I reserved it immediately – "House of Dawn" was born.

Checklist 2: How to Form a Corporation.

I knew that forming the nonprofit would be a major step and most likely, the hardest. This took awhile, so I educated myself on the formation process. This consisted of a lot of research, reading, and studying every night after I put my children to bed.

According to the U.S. Small Business Administration, there are five different types of business structures to choose from: Sole proprietorship, Partnership, Limited liability company (LLC), Corporation, or Cooperative. I had to research which one of these I needed for a nonprofit and why I needed to incorporate.

Nonprofit Nugget: There are several different types of Corporation structures, such as: C corp, S corp, B corp, Close corporation, and Nonprofit corporation. You must research all options to determine which of these structures will work best for your business.

1. You need to incorporate a nonprofit if your organization will make a profit from its activities. As long as the funds raised are related to the charitable activities of the

organization you may not have to pay state or federal taxes.

2. You need to incorporate a nonprofit if you are going to ask for donations or apply for public or private grant money.

3. If your organization does not have tax-exempt status, you may be excluded from applying for many public and private grants. Getting tax-exempt status as an organization requires that you prepare a lot of complicated paperwork and adopt rules that govern your operation.

4. Incorporate a nonprofit when you will solicit tax-deductible donations or contributions. For example, when you are granted a tax-exempt status under a 501(c)(3), gifts and donations that are given to your corporation can be deducted from the donors' federal and state income tax returns, making it easier for you to secure donations.

5. Incorporate a nonprofit when you want to limit your personal liability from the organization's activities and shield your personal assets.

These are the main reasons I didn't waste any time incorporating The House of Dawn, which occurred on April 7, 2000.

Checklist 3: How to Form a Board of Directors.

According to Mr. Mumford, my next task was to form a Board of Directors and create a mission statement. I researched how to develop a board of directors and what their roles would look like. Then I began my search to find the right people to serve.

In the initial stages of choosing my board I started out with five members consisting of family and close friends to help me get started. My daddy, sister, Jerome, the co-worker who often prayed with me in the bathroom, and my dear friend Layne who worked with me at the Clayton County Cooperative Extension.

You have to start somewhere – and I chose to start with a strong circle of support. While it's not recommended to seat family members on your board of directors, I was just starting out and needed the support of those that believed in me, my vision, and wanted to see this program serving the community just as much as I did.

Eventually, the terms for our founding board members expired. By this time House of Dawn was open for business and slowly gaining a following in the community. We had no problems finding new, independent board members willing to carry the torch and help continue moving the organization forward.

Since I was officially starting a homeless shelter for teenage mothers, I needed to find an organization that offered similar services. While I appreciated my mentor's help, he ran a women's shelter and the services I planned to provide would look very different. I was at the point where Mr. Mumford had taken me as far as he could.

Just as I had done with Treetop Learning Academy and during my volunteer stint at the Hope Shelter, I needed to learn more details about the direction my nonprofit would take. My search for a credible organization to mirror began immediately.

Chapter 7

LESSONS TO BECOME AN OVERCOMER

"I was creating something from scratch."

Multitasking became my new middle name. Between searching for new board members and looking for a compatible shelter to meet with, I had to keep educating myself. I read books late into the night after putting my children to bed and used every free waking moment during daylight hours to learn all that I could about the nonprofit world.

Checklist 4: Completing a 501(c)(3) Application. When I finally got to the point of researching how to apply for House of Dawn's 501(c)(3), I was in shock at how much was needed to complete this step, making the need to meet with a comparable nonprofit even more urgent to learn more about the operations.

The challenge? There were no programs in Clayton County that were doing what I was trying to do. Not even close. To make matters worse, there weren't even any homeless programs designed to assist teenage mothers nearby.

But one thing was clear – just like the work from home program I had developed for my nine-to-five, I was creating something from scratch. Only this concept would be so much more beneficial to the teen mothers and children I hoped to serve.

I started searching the internet in hopes of finding a likeminded nonprofit somewhere . . . anywhere. The only ones that I found close to House of Dawn's mission were located up North, so I studied various websites and even called several of them. Sadly, I wasn't able to get many answers to my questions.

What was apparent just by looking at the websites' pictures and program information is that I would need a lot of money to start this program. Strangely enough, I never considered how much this venture would cost or where the money would come from. At this point I was struggling to get the money together just to pay for House of Dawn's 501(c)(3). How was I ever going to launch such an expensive program with no seed money?

This particular challenge had me feeling really down and I was on the brink of giving up.

To lift my spirits, I made an appointment to get my hair done and told my beautician, Sandy, everything. "Gurl, I know this is what God has for me to do, but I've run into a brick wall. Doing this will take money that I just don't have and I don't see where I can possibly get it from. I may just need to give up on this idea," I digressed.

Well . . . girlfriend turned me around in that chair, looked me dead in the eyes and declared, "If God gave you the vision, HE will make the provisions – do NOT give up!" Stephanie said with so much confidence, I started to believe again. "There's money out there somewhere for such an awesome cause and necessary ministry. Maybe you should put an ad in the paper to let people know what you want to do. The right person will see it and may be willing to help; people will give to such a good cause."

The thought immediately changed my attitude, and I was ready to get back to work. I also turned my beautician's words into a mantra, saying over and over again: *if God gave you the vision, HE will make the provisions!*

I continued through the weekend, reaffirming and encouraging myself. I said that mantra so much that I finally started believing again. I had a list of "to-dos" I was ready to knock out, and Monday morning couldn't come fast enough.

First things first – I called my local newspaper, the *Clayton News Daily,* and told them what I was trying to do. I proved how much this program was needed by sharing my research on the effects of teen pregnancy and high school dropout rates in our county. I was surprised when they asked to do a story on me to learn more about my vision and what this type of program could do for young mothers in the community.

My story was printed in the local paper and while I didn't get any offers to fund my program at the time, I did get a call from the Parenting Educator at the Clayton County Cooperative Extension. They facilitated a parenting program specifically for teen parents, and she invited me to experience the class.

During this visit I was introduced to Layne, a parenting educator who led a mentoring program for the ABC's of Parenting. My prayers had been answered as I was now connected with a teen parenting program that I didn't even know existed.

I was now fulfilling the first part of my dream and passion – mentoring teen mothers – and loving every minute of it. This was not the opportunity I had been searching the World Wide Web for, but it was a chance to learn more about the needs of teen parents directly from the source, and I took full advantage of this opportunity.

My time in this program made me realize that if I was serious about doing this type of work I would have to go back to college and get my degree. When I was nineteen years old I started attending Branelle Business College to study business administration. I became a wife and new mom around the same time and chose to put family first. I eventually returned to school, but given time constraints it was difficult.

At age twenty-five I enrolled in Atlanta Metropolitan College's social work program, taking two classes a week. Meanwhile I was still working full-time, being a wife, mothering two small children (aged two and five years old), volunteered and mentored teen moms, and still struggling with Bell's Palsy which was slowly improving. Outside of getting my degree, I was still making other moves to establish House of Dawn.

To put it mildly, I was stretched thin and doing a lot more than I had ever done. But because I was slowly fulfilling my dream, I couldn't have been happier.

By 2001 I began stepping out on faith by looking at homes to fulfill my vision for House of Dawn. I still didn't have money to purchase, but thought seeing inventory would give me an idea as to what type of facility was needed. That's when Jerome mentioned Mrs. Smith, who had a suitable rental property.

When we met, I told her all about the program that I wanted to start and surprisingly, Mrs. Smith was very supportive and loved the concept. She had no problem renting me the house for such a good cause and, proceeded to give me the grand tour.

The white four-bedroom home on Main Street had space that could be converted to a fifth bedroom, and a big, unfinished basement that could be renovated into a children's day care while the moms went to school. The house even had chalkboards on the walls in the back of the house, which seemed fitting.

I knew that this house was perfect for my program; but I also knew that by the time House of Dawn was ready to open it probably wouldn't be available. I was honest with Mrs. Smith that I didn't have the funds yet but when I did, I would be back and hoped that the house would again be available.

I will never forget the first mentee I was assigned. When we met, she was seventeen years old and eight months pregnant. She and her son were my pride and joy! We worked towards completing her GED, finding her first apartment, getting her first furniture, and most importantly, being there for her in the delivery room when her son was born. The love that I had in my heart for them was unbelievable. We encouraged each other, as helping them made me even more determined to finish birthing my vision of working with teen moms.

I was finally living my passion and doing what I loved – and it didn't feel like work.

I was also blessed to have a family that loved and embraced this mission just as much as I did. It is their unselfishness that allowed them to not only share me with others, but to be able to live this dream. They were never upset when I had to unexpectedly handle an emergency that one of the moms were having, or when I had to leave home at inopportune times to be in the delivery room with a teen mom. I am blessed to have such a supportive family!

In the meantime, I was not only enjoying being a mentor, I was good at it! So much so that I was offered a part-time job as a parenting educator. Eventually I was offered a part-time job with the Clayton County Cooperative Extension. But I was afraid to leave my full-time job because I also had a financial obligation to my family. Really, I didn't want to give up the great benefits it offered in exchange for a position that was part-time and grant-funded. At the time I thought that meant keeping my day job in order to pay the bills.

As much as I wanted to take the part-time position, I wasn't ready to leave the job that still left me feeling unappreciated and unfulfilled just yet.

*   *   *

One night after putting the kids to bed, I could hear newscaster Amanda Davis' voice on Fox 5 News discussing Wednesday's Child. This news segment features foster care children looking for an adoptive home and forever family. As I entered the room, I really noticed the young girl being interviewed. My heart started beating so fast! I took one look at her and already felt like she was my child, I just needed to find her.

I called Fox 5 News the next day. Strangely, the receptionist knew nothing about the recent news segment and had never even heard of Wednesday Child, which has been airing for years. So, I began looking up Wednesday Child on the web and searching through all of the kids that were up for adoption. I continued to scroll for what seemed like forever and suddenly, I saw her face.

My heart skipped beats as I read her bio. She was twelve years old and as I continued to scroll down, discovered that she had a thirteen-year-old brother. We never considered splitting them up.

We decided that we wanted to adopt at least one child after I gave birth to our first son, Jam. We immediately took the necessary certification courses and as we were waiting for a little girl to adopt, I got pregnant with my daughter, Bria.

Because the certification lasts five years, we were already approved as adoptive parents when I saw that Wednesday's

Child segment. This blessing in disguise sped up their adoption process ever so slightly.

After months of online inquiries, telephone calls, and emails, someone finally called me back. I admittedly almost gave up a few times because of all the red tape. But six months later, we finally met them in person.

As we started the process with the Georgia Division of Family and Children Services (DFCS) in Fulton County, we were finally allowed to visit and take them for a four-hour outing. When we picked them up from their group home at Carrie Steele Pitts, they were so excited they told all their friends they were leaving with us. I remember one of my soon-to-be son's friends there asking who we were, and he casually replied, "Oh, that's my mom and dad."

That moment was confirmation that these were our kids.

Our day consisted of lunch at the mall. Bria, who was three years old at the time, wanted to get on the merry-go-round and Cameron offered to take her. We watched him hoist her up on the horse while my son Jam, then five years old, rode on the horse across from them. They seemed to share an instant bond – they were all brothers and sisters from the beginning.

In November 2001 I officially became a mother of four after adopting these two children. We now had a twelve- and thirteen-year-old as well. Life was good, but became extremely busy for me.

Once the adoption was final, I needed more flexibility in my life across the board since there were a lot of adjustments. I had to get us all acclimated to our new normal – especially our newest family members. Not only were there changes in all of our household routines, but I also found myself having to spend a lot of time at their schools getting them caught up academically.

I trimmed my college course schedule down to one class, but the corporate job was becoming more difficult to manage. These adjustments weren't giving me enough hours in a day, and I even had to stop working on House of Dawn for a while.

*   *   *

During this time, my daddy became very sick battling his second bout with cancer. One day, I went to pick him up from work and was crushed as I told him I had to put college and House of Dawn on hold because I had too many other things going on. My parents were always concerned with how busy I was: work, family, school, and all the stress that I would be under due to Bell's Palsy. And with my daddy fighting cancer for the second time I truly felt defeated, tired, and weary.

Daddy and I had so many conversations about my dream of House of Dawn and he always gave me the best advice. I remember him telling me it was okay to put House of Dawn down for a while as long as I didn't give it up completely. He always encouraged me by saying, "This work that God has for you to do will be hard. He didn't just choose anybody to do this work . . . he chose you. While it will not be easy, it will be worth it. Keep pushing! You are going to bless so many! Just keep doing what HE told you to do and keep going where HE tells you to go and HE will see you through this. House of Dawn will be a reality for you, and a home for so many moms and babies. But what I want you to do when you pick it back up is to write down all of your steps, no matter how big or how small. Write them down and work on just a couple of things at a time. When you have completed those things, check them off then move on to the next few things. Stop trying to do so much at one time! God is a God of order – He don't like no mess."

My mother also told me to start keeping a prayer journal, start writing down my prayers and checking them off as God answers them. "Start writing daily to God what you are asking him for, what you've accomplished, and who helped you accomplish it. Note your frustrations and who frustrated you and why . . . just start having daily talks with God in your prayer journal and give it all to Him."

That's when I stopped trying to keep so much in my head, started writing my vision down, and writing letters in my prayer journal daily to God. "The Bible says to write down the vision and make it plain," Mom reminded me, so I did just that and started watching God continue to move.

It got to a point where it was clear that my father was dying, and Mom needed help caring for him. As his condition worsened, my sister would help in the mornings and after working half days I would take over in the afternoon. We stayed close by my parents' side during this time. On my way home I recall crying all the way home while listening to the song "Stand" by Donnie McClurkin, every evening.

In August 2002, my father passed away. Cancer may have taken over his body, but it could never extinguish his memories or his stellar advice.

He left me with so much! So many laughs, memories, words of wisdom, and instructions. For me and for the House of Dawn.

Chapter 8

I Left My Job to Follow My Passion

"It takes faith to walk the nonprofit road."

Tyler Perry really inspires me. I think I've seen all his plays, which are always very funny and offer a good message. I don't remember which play it was, but at the end Tyler came completely out of character and spoke to the audience about the play's lessons. He talked about how far God has brought him from being homeless and sleeping in his car to producing plays in sold out theaters. Perry said, "Never give up on your dreams if God gave you a vision keep pushing even when others tell you to give up or when it seems too hard . . . if he put in your heart keep pushing."

Tyler also told the audience that he says the Prayer of Jabez daily, adding "When you start saying that prayer, God is going to start working on your behalf and you better be ready for the blessing that you are asking him for." I went and brought the book *Prayer of Jabez* so that I could understand the prayer and story that Tyler was speaking of.

Going to that corporate job during the first six months after my father passed felt like even more of a struggle. That's when Lucy, who worked at the Clayton County Cooperative Extension where I still volunteered as a mentor for teenage

30

mothers, told me she was finally going to retire and that she would love to train me for her job.

Our boss, had continued to notice my volunteer work and once again, offered me Lucy's position which was a part-time, grant-funded job with no benefits and no guarantee of continued funding. I was still afraid to leave my corporate position, but understood the grim reality that is how grant-funded programs typically work.

Yet I somehow knew that taking this position would give me just what I needed. After a family meeting, we decided this would be the best course, we would just have to spend less money for awhile. I would also have the flexibility to set my own schedule. I could have lunch with my kids at school, go on field trips, be able to stay home when they were sick, take them to doctor appointments, and so much more – all without being scolded or written up.

Knowing that God would provide for our needs, I happily resigned from my full-time job and became a Parenting Educator for teenage moms. I finally stepped out on faith and left my job to follow my passion!

And this is also where the hard work began! The Clayton County Cooperative Extension team saw the need for House of Dawn's services in our community, and they quickly became my support system.

Lucy trained me to take over her position, and I worked side by side learning as much as possible from Layne, who became my mentor. She showed me the ropes of working with teen moms, the ABC's of Parenting Program, and helped prepare me for my House of Dawn journey. I soaked up as much knowledge as I could from her.

My boss was so good about sending me to trainings that helped increase my knowledge and allowing me to sit on boards for her so that I could learn more about how they operate. She also encouraged me to share my vision about House of Dawn even when I was out on Clayton County Cooperative Extension business, which helped get me connected in the community.

This ignited my House of Dawn fire again! Taking the combined advice of my father, my mother, and Tyler Perry, I wrote down my next steps, adding them to my daily prayer journal, and ending each with the Prayer of Jabez.

"And Jabez called on the God of Israel saying, 'Oh, that You would bless me indeed, and enlarge my territory, that Your hand would be with me, and that You would keep me from evil, that I may not cause pain.' So, God granted him what he requested."

My prayers were answered after working two different part-time jobs at the Clayton County Cooperative Extension for several months. God supplied my needs as these two positions were the equivalent of a full-time job, which provided the flexibility to work while pursuing my passion. My dreams for House of Dawn were coming true.

Chapter 9

TAKING THE SERVICE ROAD

"Trying to help people shouldn't be this hard."

After a hiatus that included building and caring for my family, firming up financial resources, and just dealing with life in general, I was finally ready to finish making House of Dawn a reality. I had completed most of the necessary steps to becoming a nonprofit organization, but now it was time for me to move forward.

Still pregnant with the original idea I had in my head, I'd taken my father's advice and made a checklist of all the steps I needed to accomplish. Thanks to the Clayton County Cooperative Extension, I now had a few years of experience working with teen moms and their children AND working with teen parents in DFCS and the Department of Juvenile Justice (DJJ). The next step was to find and open a home.

For the past three years I also continued writing in my prayer journal and concentrating on researching programs that existed like the one I envisioned. Layne was already teaching me about program development, finding funding, and writing grants. I had already developed the program and the next steps on my checklist were:

☐ Finding a home for my teenage mothers to live.

☐ Finding out how much my start-up costs would be.

☐ Finding out how much operational costs would be.

☐ What else it would take to start this home?

☐ Find funding for this program.

Nonprofit Nugget: *Start-up, operational, and funding are basic needs of any business. Tailor this list to address your organization's specific needs.*

To make sure I was not getting overwhelmed, I took my tasks on five at a time and checked them off upon completion.

I finally found and contacted a similar program online. I called and the woman I spoke with was extremely helpful and nice. She shared budget information and details about the program. Before we hung up, she said, "I want to see you get this program open. The teenage girls in Clayton County need you and your program! If you are ever in Savannah, you are welcome to come visit my program. I would be glad to give you a tour and share any other information that I have." She invited me to call her back anytime for more information.

Excited and motivated, I created a new checklist with updated goals to complete. But as I checked things off, sometimes the list grew and each list got more difficult to accomplish.

I continued to research more programs doing similar work and to my surprise, there was a program like the one I wanted in Fulton County, Georgia! I enthusiastically called and spoke with the program's director, sharing what I wanted to do in Clayton County and where I was in the process. My hope was that she'd be willing to meet so that I could find out more.

But this time, the conversation went a little differently. She started out very nice and proceeded to tell me all about her program, how much support she had from funders, the community, churches, and more. She also made sure to let me know upfront that she was a Christian. I was so excited to hear all of this and asked if I could come by and see her program one day when it was convenient. I also offered to volunteer with her organization to learn the ropes of how a similar residential program operates That's when she hit me with a response that I didn't see coming.

"No!" she snapped. "I can't meet with you and you can't come here. You need to find out the hard way – just like I did."

I was flabbergasted, but thanked her for her time. Even after hearing her hang up, I just sat there holding the phone in shock. I had no idea that this field was so competitive and remember thinking to myself, *wow – does she realize she said that out loud?*

As time went on, I continued to look for likeminded programs. I also visited programs that didn't offer the same type of services that I planned to, but were group homes or residential facilities that could give me some ideas. While they were not as rude as the so-called Christian from Fulton County, they still did not want to help or share any information and I remember thinking, *it shouldn't be this hard to help people.*

I was now experiencing what is known as "the crab syndrome," and it was disheartening. I couldn't understand why we were competing with each other instead of celebrating and helping to pull one another up. Up until this point, I had some wonderful sisters in my life that were happy for me, proud of the work that I was stepping up to do, and encouraging. So, I was taken aback when the "crabs" started crawling my way. But they were out there and I had to learn to pivot, because this wouldn't be my last experience with them.

I recalled Layne telling me that the closer I got to the goal, the harder it would get. I was experiencing contractions with my House of Dawn pregnancy, and had to refocus and remember whose work I was doing. While some wouldn't help or share information, I knew God would lead me to the right people for the next part of my journey. It would get harder before it got easier, and I was now prepared for that.

About three years after House of Dawn's incorporation, I found that a network of homes for teenage mothers had been started by the Georgia Campaign for Adolescent Pregnancy Prevention (G-CAPP). After researching them, I longed to be in this network, so I reached out letting them know about House of Dawn's program.

My goal was to make sure they knew Dawn Murray and House of Dawn! I started building a relationship with them by staying in touch, networking, and attending any function G-CAPP held. Because the Extension Service had a teen parenting program, we were in the loop with G-CAPP attending all of their events. So, when I found out that they were having an open house at one of their SCHs, I had to attend.

I not only attended, but showed up with all of my Clayton County Extension team and a couple of founding board members who were supporting me in bringing this program to the community.

As we arrived, I heard a voice speaking that I would never forget, but still couldn't believe my ears. It was the same rude "Christian" executive director I spoke with phone – the same one that wouldn't let me see he wouldn't let me volunteer, wouldn't share any information, and told me to find out the hard way like she did.

All I could think was, *look at God!* This couldn't get any better! Despite her attempts to stifle my vision, I still managed to get in to see her second chance home and learn about her program thanks to G-CAPP. God was truly ordering my steps and putting the right people in my path at the right time!

G-CAPP calls homes for teen mothers and their children a "Second Chance Home" (SCH). I now had a title for this part of my vision and knew that one day House of Dawn would be a part of this G-CAPP Network I was learning so much about.

Overall the open house was great, but I still left with questions. What I needed was a one-on-one with this lady because I needed to know how much it would cost to operate one of these homes. I had licensing, zoning, and general questions about operating a Second Chance Home (SCH) and since hers was the only stand-alone home in the network at the time, she was still a wealth of information. G-CAPP referred to her agency and an agency like House of Dawn as stand-alone agencies because we were not technically under the umbrella of any agency – we were the "founders" – nor did we have the backing of a larger agency.

Months after attending G-CAPP's open house, these questions were still burning inside me. So, I said a prayer and told God I was going to call this program again and to "please not let that mean lady answer the phone," but allow someone who had a heart to help me pick up.

When I called a very nice lady answered the phone, introducing herself as the program manager. I reminded her of who I was at the open house and that I was the "tall light-skinned lady asking all of those questions" with the Clayton County group. This description helped her to remember me.

I let her know that I wanted to ask some questions about the program.

At this point, she didn't know about my previous conversation with her boss months earlier. But she did know I was invited to attend G-CAPP's open house and that we were trying to open a much-needed home for teen mothers in Clayton County. So, she graciously agreed to meet with me and answered all the questions she could and told me to call her if I needed anything else. She even wished me luck with getting the program open because there was such a need everywhere. This woman was a breath of fresh air.

During this time, I continued to build a strong relationship with G-CAPP. By this time, the program had accepted several other homes into the network and I was always sure to let them know that House of Dawn was on the rise and how badly we needed a SCH in Clayton County.

G-CAPP had funding for SCHs so the first grant that I wrote requesting funding for my program was to them. I had no idea how to write grants – I just knew the basics that I learned from Layne. I also got help from the nonprofit Hearts to Nourish Hope, one of many supporters in Clayton County that wanted to see this program succeed.

We didn't get that grant, but I continued to build the relationship and keep G-CAPP updated with House of Dawn's progress. I needed them to see how serious I was and that while it was taking a while, I was still working and not giving up.

As time went on, I found out that G-CAPP was not really interested in funding me because I was so new, had never operated a program, and was considered a stand-alone agency. All of this made me a major risk for ꜰ The other SCHs that they took into the network of bigger agencies, had plenty of experience, and around awhile. However, I was determined to show them that I could do this.

The biggest problem for me and why it was taking so long was because I had a clear vision but no money to fulfill it. Realizing how expensive it was to run these programs as well as the start-up costs, I developed a budget and set my eyes on finding "funders" that could help pay for it.

My plan was to get start-up and operational funds from G-CAPP and operational funds for teen moms that needed to be placed with their children in DFCS and DJJ. Now I just had to figure out how to start a residential program and then actually get the dollars into my hands.

Chapter 10

GETTING LICENSED

"When the going gets tough, the tough keep going."

As I continued working on my funding plan, there were still other items on my checklist to complete. I still needed to find a home, get licensed, and start writing policies and procedures.

Checklist 5: How to Get Licensed.

I knew how I wanted the program to run, but had to make sure that it would align with the Office of Regulatory Child Care (ORCC), the Georgia State licensing office. My research found that this would be a lengthy process that began with requesting a licensing packet that had a long application to submit. I also requested a funding application from DJJ and DFCS. These items were added to my prayer journal and updated checklist.

Checklist 6: How to Navigate Zoning.

Because I didn't have funding yet, I stepped out on faith and continued looking for homes for House of Dawn. While I prayed for the home I saw a few years earlier on Main Street and wrote it down in my prayer journal, it had now been rented for years.

Layne told me about a home in College Park right on the border of both Fulton and Clayton counties. When I saw it, it seemed like another home that would make a great SCH. After speaking with the owner about my plans, she said she'd be delighted to rent us the home. I then spoke with a Fulton County commissioner to see if I had any chance of getting zoned there. I was told that it was an election year, and no more group home would be zoned in his district. Needless to say, I was disappointed.

Through research, I learned quite a bit about what it would take to secure a home for this program. What I didn't know about were the zoning requirements – finding a home does no good if you can't get it zoned.

I was also realizing how political this process was going to be. I would have to learn to talk to elected officials to explain and sell my program in hopes of gaining their support. After all, that was the first step in getting community support, too. It seemed this process was getting more difficult and even painful, which only meant I was getting further along in my vision's pregnancy and experiencing more contractions.

To make things even worse, a moratorium was issued in Clayton County on group homes. This meant no more group homes would be zoned in Clayton County. I didn't know what to do at this point. However, I still didn't let that stop me from continuing with my ORCC licensing paperwork, hoping that at some point before I was ready to secure my SCH the moratorium would be lifted.

Filling out this extensive paperwork also allowed me to understand more about the requirements. That's when I truly realized I still had a big problem: the lack of MONEY! As I worked through the licensing packet, I found more major stumbling blocks:

1. I technically was not qualified to be the executive director because I didn't meet ORCC's requirements. At the time, their requirements included a masters degree or a bachelors degree with at least four years of experience. This program could not operate legally without this position being filled, so I would need a legitimate executive director that met these requirements.

Nonprofit Nuggets: *Do your research to find out the requirements from ALL governmental entities in your area prior to attempting to open your business.*

2. The home needed to be furnished with all utilities on and fully operational in order for ORCC licensing to come and inspect the property and program.

3. I had to meet Fire Marshal codes, building inspections, and county and state regulations complete with the required permits in order to even be considered for an ORCC license.

In that moment, I didn't have money to do any of these things. I asked God where to go from here. I was tired and mentally worn out, again feeling like I just needed to give up. After all, I had been at this for years and this was taking way too long! All I wanted to do was help these young moms, and I couldn't understand why it was so difficult.

Additionally, while I had many supporters, I came across many non-supporters who felt Clayton County didn't have a teen pregnancy problem. Although House of Dawn's services were obviously needed, there were people who didn't want this type of program in their community. Some smiled in my face but behind my back they were working against me. They felt I was making a fool of myself by trying to solve a problem that in their minds didn't exist.

I was often surprised to hear people who I thought were friends say, "Girl just let it go, that's nice what you want to do and all . . . your heart is in the right place, but maybe it's not meant to be. It's time for you to understand that these folks will never let you put anything in this county to help homeless pregnant young girls. It was a nice dream, but maybe it's time you moved on." All I could think was, *wow, well I won't be sharing my vision with you anymore!*

What I did understand was it was time for me to start moving in silence, only sharing the rest of this journey with a select few that God told me to share it with. I knew my friends meant well, perhaps were even trying to protect me, but "walking with" a vision meant "walking away" from some people.

All of the negativity and red tape brought me to tears many times. One particular night, I was praying and crying while writing in my prayer journal, I clearly heard God tell me, "Yes it's hard and yes it's tiring, but you aren't doing this for you – you are doing this for Me. This is My work and you will stop when I tell you to stop. Everyone won't see your vision. I gave it to you for a reason, not them." I stopped crying and praying and continued to hear these words until I fell asleep.

The next morning I got up, still dragging. I called my friend, mentor, and prayer warrior Layne, sharing my prayer and what God told me yet still feeling like I just couldn't go on.

"Do you have the faith of a mustard seed?" she asked.

When I hesitated, she sternly asked again, almost yelling. I responded, "Yes, of course, I do."

"Then I'm on the way over to your house," she said.

Layne arrived with anointing oil and prayed for the House of Dawn and me. She asked God to remove the stumbling blocks or tell me how to get over them. Layne was no joke when it came to praying! Her faith in God was so unbelievable to me. I had already learned so much from her and as she prayed, I couldn't do anything but cry. She cried with me then told me to dry my tears, ordering me to go be about our Father's business and continue the work He had for me to do.

That was the game changer . . . I was ready to get back in the ring and finish what God had for me to do. I could face my stumbling blocks head-on or jump over them.

I also thought about the advice my Daddy gave me.

First, that no weapon formed would prosper, and second, that the angels would rejoice while the devil would be angry about all the lives that would be saved through the House of Dawn. I felt awakened and enlightened.

Once again, I made a checklist of everything I still had to do. After all, God was a God of order; He doesn't like "mess." I made a checklist of my stumbling blocks and started planning one-by-one how to tackle them.

The first one was not being qualified to be the director. It was very unlikely I could go back to school now and get my degree in time to open the House of Dawn. And in the midst of all that I was already doing, I couldn't even make time for that right now. I knew I would definitely have to go back and do it as soon as I could. But I felt it was more important for me to move closer to birthing this House of Dawn baby than to stop for school. I felt like I was in my last trimester and I had to keep going.

I decided to ask the ORCC what was the alternative was if I didn't have the qualifications to be the executive director. The lady I spoke with said I could just hire a director, all I needed was the right person with the right degree and qualifications. Then I had to think who could I get that would agree to be the director before there was even money coming into the program to pay them. I would worry about how I could pay the person later but, in that moment, I prayed for God to send an executive director to move House of Dawn forward.

Next, I still didn't have any start-up money. G-CAPP already said I was too much of a risk being a new stand-alone agency. But if I opened and got licensed, they would consider funding me to apply for the next grant that was coming out.

There was still the problem of Clayton County's self-imposed moratorium on group homes. So, I decided to speak with the commissioners again and ask if there were any alternatives for this situation. One commissioner told me that while they had no idea how long the moratorium would last, I could always look at homes within the city limits. "This program is needed, so keep pushing," she counseled. So, while I was unable to zone in the county, I set new sights on the cities.

Chapter 11

STEPPING INTO OUR SECOND CHANCE

One morning after getting the kids off to school, the phone rang as I sat down at my desk. The caller introduced herself as Yvonne Prioleau and reminded me that we previously met at the G-CAPP open house. I instantly remembered she was the program manager who graciously answered my questions and shared information with me.

Checklist 7: Steps to Building a SCH.

During our conversation, Yvonne let me know that she was no longer working for the SCH. She also mentioned how much she missed working with teen moms and asked if I had opened my SCH home yet. I shared that we were progressing but still tackling some of the stumbling blocks we'd encountered. Yvonne knew a lot about running SCH operations and amazingly, offered to assist in any way that she could. She said she would even volunteer to help get House of Dawn up and running.

My prayer had just been answered! I quickly shared the degree and qualifications that ORCC required. I explained that I did not have my degree yet, but planned to return to school once House of Dawn opened – all I needed was an executive director.

"Well, you just found one," Yvonne said. "I meet all of ORCC's requirements and would love to go back to working with teenage mothers. And I would love to be your executive director!"

Those words were music to my ears! I accepted her offer and we immediately went to work on finishing up the licensing packet.

At the time, we both worked day jobs. Usually after I put the kids to bed we would develop the ORCC licensing packet, conversing back and forth on policy and procedures. Throughout this process, Yvonne volunteered her time and burned the midnight oil with me until the packet was complete.

Although there were other stumbling blocks lying before me, I was still very encouraged. I knew if God had sent a qualified executive director willing to work without pay in the interim, He would answer my prayers that would make House of Dawn a reality.

* * *

My search for a home was also officially "on." We were denied the home in College Park so that was out. No group homes could be established in Clayton County due to the moratorium, so that was out. With no way to remove these obstacles, I just prayed and asked God for direction. All I knew was that I had to find a home and figure out how to pay for it. Of course, that also meant bringing the home up to code as required by the state, city, and county governments – which would take money. Since we were denied start-up funds from G-CAPP, I knew I had to wait for God to show me how to proceed.

It was time to start thinking outside the box for ways to bring this vision to life. Perhaps finding a house, paying for it ourselves, then bringing it up to code later was the solution. This would have been an expensive workaround for our family, but I knew once House of Dawn was operational it would all be worth it.

It just so happened that Jerome cut Mrs. Smith's grass earlier that week and noticed a "for rent" sign was back up in her yard. This was the very first home we believed to be the perfect location four years earlier.

My thoughts wouldn't let me sleep that night. When we first met Mrs. Smith she was so supportive of my vision for House of Dawn . . . would she still feel the same way? I could clearly see the chalkboards on the walls, could hear laughter coming from the basement that would convert to a day care for the children while their moms went to school, and all the other finishing touches that would make this House of Dawn's home. The fact that the same house I thought perfect years ago was again available could only be God working.

Once morning arrived, I couldn't get there fast enough. Mrs. Smith opened the door and warmly greeted me with her bright smile and snow-white hair that always looked like she just left the salon. "I often thought about you and wondered whatever happened with the nice little program that you wanted to start to help those young moms," she said after inviting me in.

I excitedly explained that I'd used the time away to research, plan, and learn how to operate the program correctly. I talked about how learning how to start my nonprofit, operate the program correctly, and setting up the business portion had been a rough journey.

I clarified how making sure the home was located in the city limits and not the county was the only way for us to get approved by the zoning authority. It took more time than I initially thought, but I was ready to rent a house for my program.

Mrs. Smith smiled and said, "Well, my house is located in the city limits and my house next door for rent is in the city limits; the county line starts at the end of the driveway of the house next door so technically, that house is also within the city limits."

"This house must be meant for you," Mrs. Smith said, agreeing to not show the house to anyone else as we went through the zoning process. She also graciously agreed that I did not have to pay rent until the zoning issue was resolved. She didn't even require me to put any money down.

Won't He do it! My daddy told me this program was going to be put together in such a way that only God can get the glory and boy, was he right!

Turns out that the house was inside of the city limits and everything Mrs. Smith said about where the county line was drawn was correct. This was crazy and too good to be true! Of course, I still had no start-up funds, no money to get through the zoning process, no money to pay Mrs. Smith's rent once it did get zoned, nor the money to pay to bring it up to code.

But the faith of a mustard seed had gotten me this far. I immediately began praying about getting the house through zoning and I'd cross the other roads once I got to them.

*　　*　　*

As it turns out, this was a very old home. A lot of work would be needed not only to bring it up to code, but to create the environment I visualized for young mothers and their children.

Naysayers also claimed that the house would never pass inspection or even capable of being brought up to code. In addition, I was again told the program wasn't needed nor welcome in this community.

I pressed on through all of the negative talk, knowing that this had to be the home for us. After touring it four years ago, I prayed and noted it all in my prayer journal. I also continued following my daddy's instructions and made a checklist. My next tasks were:

- ☐ Go to City Hall (or in your case, whatever government office handles this) to find out what the requirements were to start a group home.

- ☐ Find out the zoning policy.

- ☐ Get fire code regulations.

- ☐ See what is needed to bring the home (building, etc.) up to code for state licensing.

- ☐ Develop a start-up budget.

- ☐ Figure out how to pay for all of this and/or where the money will come from.

Nonprofit Nugget: *Most of these are basic needs when your business will operate out of a commercial building or facility. Tailor this list to address your organization's specific needs.*

As the next leg of this journey began, I recognized that I was in the last trimester with my House of Dawn "baby". Yes, this pregnancy just kept getting harder, but I was still up for the challenge. I had come too far to turn back now.

I knew what was needed after developing the budget, but it cost even more than this by the time we finished meeting the requirements. Keep in mind these are the prices we paid fifteen years ago, today's pricing (and potentially some of the requirements) will cost more today:

☐ Zoning application: $350.

   Your cost is: $_____

☐ Fire inspection: $482.

   Your cost is: $_____

☐ Fire alarm system: $5,420.

   Your cost is: $_____

☐ Sprinkler system: $8,305.

   Your cost is: $_____

☐ Fire suppression system in the stove hood range: $983.

   Your cost is: $_____

☐ Renovations to bring facility to code: $7,000 (this number was based on some of the work being completed with in-kind donations and volunteer hours.)

   Your cost is: $_____

☐ Rent: $7,000 (we paid $1,000 per month and budgeted in seven months of rental payments.)

   Your cost is: $_____

Nonprofit Nugget: *You also have to allot money for unforeseen expenses. For example, the first time we submitted our zoning application we got denied. This meant that we had to pay another $350 to resubmit the application just to have a chance to go before the Zoning Committee – with no guarantee of success. There are certain things, like zoning, that you will have to pay each time you apply regardless of the circumstances. We also ended up paying about five months rent out of pocket once we exhausted the money we budgeted for rent.*

So for starters, I needed about $30,000 minimum. Not having these funds at my disposal turned this journey into a heck of a learning experience. God was truly ordering my steps and my words.

I barely had the $700 zoning fee so I researched while carefully completing the application and all of its requirements myself because I didn't have money to pay an attorney.

In March 2004, the zoning sign went up in Mrs. Smith's front yard, which was very scary for me. I was told that once that sign went up, the neighbors, community, or anyone in the city that would be against us having this program there could show up at the zoning meeting to protest – and some did protest.

What worked to our benefit was that the closest neighbors to the home were siblings of Mrs. Smith. She assured me that they wouldn't fight us and we had their support.

Nevertheless, I went door-to-door selling the program by visiting the neighbors, nearby businesses, and major stakeholders to explain the positive impacts and life-saving services House of Dawn would bring to young mothers and babies. I needed to personally clear up any misconceptions, stereotypes, and rumors about the new home for teenage mothers.

I heard a chorus of negative things, such as: "There goes the neighborhood!" "All those young girls will bring a bunch of young boys hanging around the house." "Our property values will go down once you move in." "They shouldn't have had a baby if they couldn't afford it." "We don't need that program here; we don't have a problem with teen pregnancy."

This list of complaints, assumptions, and rumors were the things I had to defuse. First, Jerome was the one who kept up the landscaping at that house all these years, and he would continue to do so. Second, this home would have 24-hour supervision so there wouldn't be boys hanging around. As a matter of fact, this house would offer better supervision than most private homes had. Most importantly, I educated anyone who would listen about the fact that Clayton County owned one of the highest teen pregnancy rates in the state of Georgia, so the program was definitely needed.

What people also did not realize was alongside the list of complaints came the constant cries for help that were being ignored.

I would get calls at all hours of the day and night from homeless teenage mothers in need of a safe haven, crying because they had nowhere to go or had to stay in homes where they were abused. Some young mothers didn't have any support at all, asking me weekly if I had opened the new home yet because they were being put out and had nowhere to go. Some had to drop out of high school because they had no one to keep their baby. Some even asked if they could stay with me! This program and its services were definitely needed in this community, and I was determined to bring it here!

Fortunately, I had supporters from the Clayton County Cooperative Extension, Mrs. Smith, many in the community at large, and G-CAPP (our soon to be funder), all who attended the zoning meeting to support House of Dawn.

But what was really poignant was the homeowner of an SCH in Dalton, Georgia who drove a little over one hundred miles to speak on my behalf. This man literally donated his house for this worthy cause. He explained that this house was not a threat to the neighborhood, but a good thing to have in the community. He wanted to share that these girls caused no problems in Dalton and in fact, they were welcomed to and by the community. Mrs. Smith also spoke in our favor, assuring that this program wouldn't pose a threat and was welcomed in the community by she and her siblings, who would be our immediate neighbors.

Soon the wait was over as House of Dawn passed zoning! A SCH was officially coming to Clayton County!

Now that we were zoned, it was time to start paying $1,000 a month for rent.

Since we were about to devote a lot of money to bring this home to code for the city and state and all that entailed, as well as setting up the business, we would need a long-term lease to protect our investment. Mrs. Smith understood this and gave us the long-term lease we requested instead of a yearly lease.

Chapter 12

MAKING HOUSE OF DAWN A HOME

Now that we officially had a home, I had to get it up to code in order to receive a certificate of occupancy and business license from the city. These items were mandatory in order to get a state license to operate from the ORCC. That license would allow us to get a G-CAPP grant and a contract with the Department of Human Services (DHS). These were House of Dawn's two initial funding sources, so I still had to complete all of these steps in order to open and operate this program.

With each new step, came new requirements. I had to have:

- A six-foot privacy fence put up in the backyard.

- Four-foot hedges around the parking lot.

- Handicap ramps.

- A handicap parking sign and everything needed to make it ADA compliant.

- A fire suppression system in the hood of the stove.

- Money to pay the fire and building inspectors.

Nonprofit Nugget: *While you can't find out requirements for things like fencing, landscaping, and handicap access until you choose a home, you may be able to get information about the cost for fire and building inspectors beforehand.*

All this and I still had to furnish and decorate the house. Despite the rising start-up budget all I could think of was what Sandy told me while doing my hair years earlier: if God gave you the vision, HE will make the provisions!

This is a business, so I considered applying for a business loan. But it is also new and unproven, which no one would loan me $30,000 to start. That's when I received a mailer from Chase Bank about obtaining a home equity line of credit and knew I had just been given the provision.

I talked with Jerome about my plan, which began with taking out a home equity line of credit on our home in order to make a business loan to House of Dawn for start-up costs. Once we were up and running, I would host fundraisers to pay off this debt of start up cost. He agreed and the next day I applied for the home equity line of credit.

Remarkably, House of Dawn was now prepared for the projected $30,000 worth of expenses, which also happened to be the maximum amount that we could borrow. What I wasn't prepared for were the additional costs and the unexpected conditions that the city required. Every time I thought we had completed what was asked of us, they would give me something else to do that came with a big price tag. These things were not listed in the paperwork nor required by the county – they were just unexpected demands that I wasn't financially prepared for.

After exhausting our home equity line of credit, I started applying for credit cards to keep this vision alive. I had come too far to turn back now so I didn't have a choice but to keep going and keep praying.

The bright side was working on the house, and seeing its progress always made me excited. Jerome spent long nights – sometimes even overnight – finishing the basement expected to be a day care area for the kids along with a very small administrative office with just enough room for two desks, files, and Yvonne and I.

That's when the city informed me that we could not use the basement for our day care, not even for the four babies expected to live in the home. They also said that we would have to be licensed to operate a child care center. The group home license was a separate entity, and we couldn't have two different licenses in the same building. Alternatively, we decided to turn the basement into our administrative space and place the babies in a nearby day care. Yvonne and I would share an office, and other offices were created for future hires.

And just when I thought the worst was over, we discovered that we had not yet weathered the worst storm.

The city told us that they did not employ a fire inspector to inspect the facility, and finding one was going to take time. The wait was excruciating, but eventually they engaged a fire inspector from Braselton, Georgia who was our worst nightmare!

Despite bringing the house to code, completing the city's requirements (and then some), as well as requirements listed in the inspector's own paperwork, he kept adding more items and seemed to make things up as he went along. Exhausted and frustrated, I kept applying for more credit cards to keep up with incoming expenses. It was also heartbreaking to have paid rent and utilities for several months on an empty house.

After getting through that agonizing process in 2004, we finally passed inspection and received our certificate of occupancy and business license! Now we could finally submit the licensing paperwork that Yvonne and I had worked so hard on to ORCC. This is when we discovered there was a six-month waiting list just for them to come out and inspect our home.

Again, everyone who had worked so hard to make House of Dawn a reality was very disappointed . . . but what else could we do? We had no choice but to continue paying rent and utilities on an empty house. In the meantime, Yvonne's familiarity with audits and site visits ensured that the house was ready for ORCC inspection. Throughout this process Yvonne and I became very close – she was like a second mother to me and we made a great team!

We also decorated the home, which really brought to fruition the vision God had given me nearly five years earlier. I wanted this to be the home that many of the girls who would come through the program never had. I wanted the rooms painted in pretty, bright, girly colors, with beautiful curtains, and comforters, and really cute baby beds!

The common areas needed to feel very warm and cozy. I could picture them sitting in the living room with their babies laughing and talking – a baby in a bouncer, a baby in a swing, another baby being held by her mom – all very relaxed and laid back. And at dinnertime, the house mom would have cooked them a wonderful meal and they all would come sit at the dining room table, bless the food, and enjoy a family-style feast.

I envisioned the girls doing their chores together while the house mom would look after the babies. When it was bedtime, the house mom would assist the young moms with bathing their babies while encouraging their nurturing and bonding time. The babies would enjoy their baths and their moms would go into their rooms and rock their babies to sleep. I planned to provide glider rockers or rocking chairs in every room to make sure this could happen. The babies would be down by 8:00 p.m. allowing the moms to have some "me" time. I pictured them watching movies with the house mom, playing games, or just listening to music – whatever they wanted to do to relax before they had to prepare for the next day and hit the bed themselves.

This had been my vision for the last five years, so Yvonne set up a house schedule to ensure these kinds of things would happen daily and that this vision would be carried out by the staff who would one day work at House of Dawn. Even though it was just the two of us for now, we looked further into the future, seeing what this now empty house could become.

We still had a few big hurdles to clear, but could already hear the laughter of young moms and the coos of contented babies. The two of us pressed on for the ORCC license and contracts to bring in operational funds to make the House of Dawn's vision a reality.

Chapter 13

TRADING SPACES VISITS CLAYTON COUNTY

After spending so much money bringing the house to code and all the unplanned "extras", I didn't have enough money to decorate as I wanted. I described this house for the last four years as my very own "Little Doll House" and it had to look a certain way – a beautiful home with bright colors and nice, comfortable furniture. The furniture and decor didn't have to be new, but it needed to be nice and/or gently used. I already knew that I would not have my girls and babies lay their heads any place I wouldn't allow my children or I to lay our heads. So, this had to be done the right the way . . . the way God showed it to me.

We were now six months into the process of opening. Since it took longer than expected for House of Dawn to open, the rumor mill began declaring that we couldn't do it. People said to my face, "I told you that community would never let this program come here!" Business colleagues said "They are not going to let you open in that community, you're just wasting your time and money." I would run into people while I was out and about who would ask (some already knowing the answer), "Wow, you're *still* not open?" Friends again started telling me to "just face it" and advised that maybe it was time to let the idea go.

House of Dawn had been my dream for nearly five years. I had gone into debt and exhausted all financial resources. I had been paying rent and utilities on an empty house for six months. It would've been easier to give up or convince myself that maybe I misunderstood the vision.

But I was still getting calls from young mothers who needed help, looking for a place to call home. Even at a snail's pace, things were moving in the right direction – forward. I knew in my heart that God didn't bring us this far to leave us now.

So, I stopped talking to certain people about House of Dawn. It had become very clear that everyone doesn't share the vision God gives, and I had to remember that He gave it to me, not to everyone else. From then on, I only shared the ups and downs of my progress with people who had encouraged me over the years; those I knew were for me and supported this program.

We continued searching for funding while waiting to open, and was about to apply for our first grant from a financial institution. My mentor Layne – who was also a House of Dawn founding board member – had started showing me how to properly fill out some smaller grant applications. She had successfully written grants for her program, AWESOME Inc. as well as for the Clayton County Cooperative Extension office where we worked together. With her help, I gave it a shot and stayed up all night applying for this one grant. The whole time I thought to myself, *this is hard, and so much work, I may have to pay someone to write my grants.*

I did get that grant finished but unfortunately, House of Dawn was not awarded. In reading it, Layne felt it was a good, well written grant. She also told me that grant writing takes a lot of work, but you win some, you lose some – it comes with the territory.

In the meantime, I had come up with a unique way to get the house decorated! One night during my prayer and journaling time, I asked God how was I going to get this done the way I wanted and the way that He showed me. I would purchase nice items here and there from yard sales when I could, people had started donating some furniture, and we made it all look really nice – but still had a way to go. What we had could pass ORCC requirements, but it wasn't decorated how I envisioned it.

I was out of money so I thought while churches won't fund the program, maybe they would help with a volunteer project. I was unable to get assistance, primarily because House of Dawn was still so new. It also didn't even occur to me that I had no credibility since the program wasn't yet operational. This was compounded by the fact that some people doubted we would open at all. Nevertheless, the next morning I visited Shiloh Baptist Church, which was right around the corner from the home. My hope was that my chances of success would be better with this smaller congregation.

Before entering the church office, I prayed. I walked in, introduced myself to the church secretary, and told her about House of Dawn. Her excitement allowed me to share information about our SCH Adopt-a-Room Program. This meant that organizations would paint, furnish, and fully decorate the room to make it their own. She loved the idea and promised to speak with the women's ministry. Eventually, she called to say that all of the women were excited and ready! They just needed to know when I could show them the home.

And just like that, House of Dawn's first Adopt-a-Room program was born. Shiloh Baptist Church decorated one of the rooms with gently-used items, and it was beautiful.

I invited other churches and women's groups to participate; the next group that adopted a room was the Clayton County Jack and Jill Club. The house was now about halfway furnished and decorated, so I continued the search for more groups to help.

By December 2004, Layne let me know that the Atlanta Community ToolBank was accepting applications for organizations who needed rooms painted as part of their Martin Luther King Day celebration. She said she would apply on House of Dawn's behalf. About a week later they accepted our application, but they had an even better offer. The television show *Trading Spaces* would soon be filming in College Park, Georgia and wanted to do a community service project for Christmas while they were here. They would need a grant proposal right away because they were about to close out their Request for Proposal (RFP).

Layne called me screaming with excitement, and I emailed her the grant application that I had just submitted – and lost – about a month earlier. I immediately knew that God had me stay up all night to write that proposal not for the finance company it was submitted to, but for this opportunity with *Trading Spaces*.

I sent her the proposal right away and we got a call two days later saying that House of Dawn had been accepted. The show's producer and his team needed to meet with us and see the house ASAP because they had to move fast. The entire *Trading Spaces* team was flying to Atlanta the next day.

All I could think was that this was too good to be true . . . my Little Doll House was about to be furnished with the vision God had given me over four years ago. And House of Dawn – the program many had said would never happen – was about be on one of the biggest shows on network television.

There was so much excitement in the air! Once I shared my vision with the *Trading Spaces* team they took it from there – taking measurements, pictures, etc. I couldn't believe my eyes. They said they would finish painting and decorating the rooms and provide any furniture that we didn't already have. They returned two weeks later with their entire team to finish the project and put up a Christmas tree. We would then have a Christmas party at the house complete with gifts for teen moms and babies.

This was all beyond amazing, and needless to say, I was on my knees thanking and praising GOD!

I again remembered Sandy's words: "If God gave you the vision, HE will make the provisions – do NOT give up! Keep doing what He told you to do." He had ordered my steps and words, and House of Dawn was the beneficiary.

I ran next door to tell Mrs. Smith, who joined in my excitement. That's when I decided to go back to the city, hoping they would be more accepting of the program now. For the first time ever, *Trading Spaces* was coming to Clayton County!

I couldn't get there fast enough. But after sharing news about the home makeover, once again I was let down as they informed me that *Trading Spaces* couldn't touch anything in that house without a permit.

I explained that they weren't doing structural work; they would only be painting and decorating. They reiterated I had to apply for a permit and could not promise that it would be approved prior to the *Trading Spaces* team's arrival in two weeks.

I remember thinking that I shouldn't have told them anything. I should have just allowed the show to come and do the work and ask for forgiveness later. Deflated, I kept the faith that this would all work out, so I followed protocol and immediately applied for the permit.

I called Layne and gave her an earful filled with cussing and yelling because at this point, I was exhausted and completely fed up. And once again, Layne came to my rescue with her anointing oil. She calmed me down and started praying for me, House of Dawn, and even the city.

*   *   *

A week passed and I still didn't have the permit. I visited the city's office almost every day, only for them to say it had not been approved yet.

About three days before *Trading Spaces* was set to arrive, I shared with Mrs. Smith that I was really getting nervous waiting on the permit. She felt my pain – here was an awesome opportunity to not only get the remaining work done on the home free of charge but to finally get the program started, and we might not be able to take advantage of it! This also benefited her since the renovations would increase the home's value.

"It's none of my business, but if you don't mind, I would like to go down there and give them a piece of my mind," asked Mrs. Smith, who was well respected in the city.

I needed and appreciated any help I could get so as not to cancel an amazing opportunity simply because I didn't have a permit allowing *Trading Spaces* to paint and decorate.

The always-composed Mrs. Smith grabbed her purse and placed it on her arm, checked her always beautiful snow-white hair in the mirror, and told me to come on. We jumped in her big blue Cadillac and went to City Hall. I was thirty-two years old but, suddenly felt like a little kid.

When we arrived, Mrs. Smith swung open the door like she owned the place. I just followed behind and waited for her to do the talking. The look on the faces of the staff told me they knew she was upset as the lady sitting at the front desk quickly said, "Yes ma'am, Mrs. Smith – how can I help you?"

"I don't like the way you all have been treating my friend," Mrs. Smith replied getting right to the point. "You all are being unfair and downright mean. *Trading Spaces* is coming here in three days to remodel the house I own that she is renting. I want to talk to someone today and find out why this girl can't have a permit."

When she turned towards the sitting area I followed, as we sat down and waited for someone to come to the lobby. The woman who came out asked me several questions about the program and the home, as well as the work that *Trading Spaces* would be doing. I answered all of the questions without hesitation.

Mrs. Smith told them, "As you can see, she has done all of her homework."

That's when we found out the permit application had not even been looked at yet. The woman disappeared again, and I prayed as we waited.

She quickly reappeared, permit in hand. We were told to keep it posted while *Trading Spaces* was on the premises. After taking the permit, all I could do was hug Mrs. Smith hard! We would have not gotten that permit in time if it hadn't been for her.

*   *   *

The day *Trading Spaces* filmed turned out to be one of the coldest days Georgia had experienced all year, but I hardly felt it as we headed to House of Dawn to await their team.

Suddenly a humongous trailer pulled up! Cars and trucks filled the driveway along with volunteers from "Hands on, Atlanta." People were everywhere as they jumped out of vehicles from all directions. They had a plan and were all in sync moving quickly and separately but together!

The house was suddenly filled to capacity as they held a meeting around our makeshift dining room consisting of a folding table draped in a beautiful tablecloth with place settings. Hey, sometimes, you have to fake it until you make it!

Once they realized it was actually a folding table, they started talking and making more notes. I was momentarily embarrassed, but suddenly they broke out into teams and took my two oldest kids with them. Others took off to Home Depot and Anna Linens. My kids were so excited as the team ran through the stores wildly purchasing wood, paint, light fixtures, appliances, bedding, and all kinds of decorative items.

I looked around and noticed there were so many people accumulating inside and out. These were not just *Trading Spaces* folks, but all of my family, friends, supporters, G-CAPP representatives, and believe it or not – strangers! Unexpectedly, people who rode by and saw the *Trading Spaces* trailer stopped, took off their coats and started working. For the first time, the community had come together for House of Dawn and worked on one accord to see it become a reality!

The awesome feeling of togetherness and unity flowing throughout the home inside and out was incredible! The fact that it was freezing cold didn't even matter, as we all were truly living in the moment. *Trading Spaces* was close to finishing the home which looked absolutely beautiful and I was standing in the middle, watching vision that I carried for nearly five years come to life.

All the appliances and light fixtures throughout the house were upgraded. They had each room decorated and painted so pretty with decor you wouldn't find elsewhere. As promised whatever furniture we didn't have, they provided and refinished what we did have making it look brand new.

They even made us a beautiful dining room set that seated six, along with some bedroom furniture including headboards.

My Little Doll House was now complete, and every room was stunning. I couldn't believe my eyes, as tears of joy streamed down my face. It was truly a day to remember.

Next up was the Christmas Party, and we had invited moms and babies from the Clayton County Cooperative Extension teen parenting program where I worked. They arrived to enjoy food, snacks, punch, and so many Christmas gifts under the tree for the moms and babies. With their trailer sitting in the front yard, word had spread all over Clayton County that *Trading Spaces* was at House of Dawn on Main Street, and people came from all over to see the home and to be a part of this experience.

Suddenly, another truck pulled up and I couldn't believe it when Santa Claus hopped out of it. The nearby Lions Club had been having a toy drive for some community children and apparently, Santa had just got off duty. On his way back to the North Pole he saw the *Trading Spaces* trailer and stopped by. We invited him in and it was perfect as our moms and babies took plenty of pictures. To finish off this magnificent day, it suddenly started snowing which just does not happen too often in Georgia.

We were now sitting in my Little Doll House, listening to Christmas carols, having a Christmas party with Santa Claus, young moms and babies, and beautiful snow falling outside . . . it was a perfect ending with so many people making my dream of bringing the first SCH to Clayton County a reality!

In December 2004, we went from being an idea to becoming known in the community thanks in part to the *Clayton News Daily*, *The Atlanta Journal-Constitution and other media outlets*. And of course, our episode was broadcast nationally on the Trading Spaces television show.

Know that what God has for you is for you . . . it will happen in *His* time!

And it all played out just like daddy always said: *God is going to do this thing in such a way that nobody could get the credit but Him!*

With the Little Doll House complete, I now just needed some "dolls" to make it a home.

* * *

About a month later, things began to really fall into place when I received a call stating the Office of Regulatory Services (ORS) would be coming out to audit our program. We waited six months for our ORS audit and were prepared.

The morning of the audit, I nervously awaited our surveyor and couldn't wait to get to the house. I was so nervous because I didn't know what to expect but I had Yvonne – who had been through audits and knew exactly what to expect.

When the surveyor rang the bell I invited her in and politely offered coffee or tea, to which she responded: "I don't take bribes."

I was outdone. Who thought good manners and Southern hospitality would ever be perceived as a bribe? *Well damn*, I thought to myself.

We all sat down at our new dining room table built by *Trading Spaces* and waited for her to comment on how beautiful the home was decorated. Instead she started looking for – and finding – anything considered to be a violation.

I couldn't believe my eyes and ears! The house was perfectly decorated for our moms and babies. But the surveyor wasn't impressed with our major renovation and after completing the inspection, gave us a list of everything that had to be corrected. Which also meant we failed the inspection.

That's when she took another look around. "It's pretty, but it isn't safe. I'll come back after you have completed everything on this list. You'll need to do a plan of correction and resubmit it. Oh, and our office is backed up so it may take a while, but I'll call and let you know when I can come back out."

A few of the things on the list were:

- An end table with a lamp on it. With this being a home for children, a child could knock the lamp over and hurt themselves.

- One of the cribs had the beautiful netting hanging from the ceiling and the netting draped the back of the crib. We had to remove the netting because a child could stand up in the crib and pull the netting down on themselves.

- Each baby crib had pretty bedding and bumper pads in them; we had to remove all of them.

Yvonne and I went through the home and removed anything that was, as the surveyor put it, pretty but unsafe. It literally took us about thirty minutes to correct these cosmetic issues. I definitely understood why we had to make those changes and wasn't upset.

What did bother me was without a license to operate, we couldn't help those young moms and babies who needed the services our home offered. I also needed my funding to start with G-CAPP because I was still paying the home's rent and utilities out of my pocket. Our home equity line of credit and credit cards were all maxed out.

It was a long three months but when she returned, we passed our home inspection and having finally had been issued our license, we were ready to operate!

I remember just standing in the living room, thanking God that after five long years, we finally had a license to operate from the state. I notified the rest of the board members and asked Layne to call Sister Ingram. I needed all my prayer warriors to come bless the house and anoint every room before we opened. I had no doubt that this home would always be blessed.

Chapter 14

THE RENT IS TOO #!@HIGH

One morning I was reviewing our profit and loss statement in preparation for House of Dawn's 2011 audit. When I got down to the leasing section, I realized we had spent approximately $80,000 in rent the previous year. We were receiving grant money to pay for it, but my inner voice still chimed in: *Self, this is not a prudent use of our resources; we are spending way too much money to rent properties that will never be ours. This money could be better spent on operations for the program. We could really cut our expenses by owning our own properties.*

This would mean we didn't have to move every time our rented home or apartment complex was under new management. Ultimately it would also be a much safer, controlled environment, and save the agency money.

In that moment, my intention was that House of Dawn would own all of its properties and I felt we should start with the Transitional Living Program (TLP). I started researching the best ways we could purchase and what the loan process was like. I discovered that hardly any banks would loan directly to a nonprofit, so I would have to personally guarantee the loan. This meant that I needed an excellent credit score . . . which I knew I did not have.

I also started looking at and pricing multi-dwelling properties that would best accommodate the families we serve. We were already leasing eight apartments, so I figured if we could purchase a multi-dwelling with eight to ten apartments, it would allow us to serve more families for less money.

Now I just had to convince the board that owning was the preferred option. It seemed to be a no-brainer to me and the board was usually supportive of my ideas, but this was a pretty big step. Knowing I had to have all my ducks in a row, I gathered all of my research and started preparing an effective presentation for the board.

*   *   *

One day while sitting at the traffic light I saw a sign advertising "Credit Repair." I wrote the telephone number down, called and spoke to a lady name Michele. I told her that I was looking to improve my credit score in order to purchase a property, and she allowed me to come in right away. I detoured to Michele's office, which ended up being located in her husband's used car dealership. Unsure if this place was professional or bootleg, I began to wonder if I should even go inside and trust this person with my social security number.

I figured hearing her out couldn't hurt and after talking for awhile, I suddenly started to feel really comfortable. Michele explained that she used to do this work from her home office and was now moving into a commercial setting because her business was starting to grow. Feeling like we needed to support each other, I decided to give her a try.

Turns out Michele knew her stuff. She pulled my score and saw that I didn't have bad credit after all. Mostly items that could be removed, some that shouldn't be there, and a couple of late payments which pulled my score down. Overall, I had good credit, she just needed to write letters to get those items removed. Michele advised what I needed to do on my end to improve my score and I did everything that she told me to do. Within six months my credit score had risen from 650 to 787. This put me in position to personally guarantee a loan for House of Dawn.

I planned and positioned myself for six months before taking this idea to the board. I wanted to make sure that I already had answers for any questions they might ask, all I's dotted and T's crossed.

Checklist 6: How to Create a Fundraising Plan.
I had also been researching and planning how we would fund this project. I made a list of potential grants that I could apply for and added them to my fundraising plan. Some items that need to be included in a fundraising plan are:

- ☐ Create your case for support.

- ☐ Identify supporters.

- ☐ Identify funding prospects.

- ☐ Determine how much you can apply for with each grant.

- ☐ Develop action steps.

- ☐ Develop your plan.

- ☐ Set fundraising goals.

- ☐ Set donor acquisition goals.

- ☐ Set reminders for when the grant is due.

☐ Who is the contact person(s).

☐ Instructions on grant delivery.

☐ Set your timelines.

☐ Determine who is accountable for what task.

Nonprofit Nugget: *A fundraising plan is a document that organizes all of your fundraising activities and objectives. Your plan should include any goals the business sets for the next twelve months, minimum. This plan usually includes the different types of fundraising that you plan to do and any grants that you would like to apply for.*

Now I felt ready to present to the board. My detailed PowerPoint presentation included the cost of rent for our SCH, administrative office, and leasing from Brooks Crossing Apartments. I showed how much we could save by purchasing, the benefits it would give the agency along with the moms and babies, the pros the cons, and of course the biggest obstacle – how we would pay for it.

We all knew how much House of Dawn paid individually for each program but when you put it all together, they couldn't help but agree that it would be in our program's best interest to purchase a facility for the TLP.

We also decided to update our strategic plan to include the purchase of all of our homes. We would start by purchasing a home for the TLP and eventually work on purchasing a property for the SCH. We already owned a home in Riverdale which was part of our Independent Living Program, so we had one down with two more to go.

The board unanimously voted to start the process of looking for a new home for the TLP and I got a real estate agent to help us find a place. I also started out by applying for three different grants one of them being our Community Development Block Grant (CDBG) for acquisition of property, which is the funder who awarded us $175,000. If this wasn't enough to pay cash up front, it would definitely get us to the closing table.

I continued looking specifically for multi-dwelling or quad units with four or five apartments. Every apartment complex we were in would rent the apartments together so that the moms in the program could be neighbors, form a bond, and be able to support each other. It would also make it more accessible for the life coach and staff. I liked this idea, as well as looking at some duplexes located on the same street in Riverdale in an attempt to keep our properties within close proximity of each other.

There was plenty of trial and error with finding the right property. We tried a few duplexes and they fell through. We even lost earnest money a couple of times. We found another apartment complex in Riverdale that was bigger than I had planned and even had room for the program to grow, which would have been great. We put down earnest money and started the loan process that went on for approximately six months before we finally got preapproved. Then the sellers of the property raised their price, asking for more than the property was valued at.

We also discovered that the pre-approval was in my name instead of House of Dawn. The loan company knew from the beginning that the loan had to be in House of Dawn's name since that's where the down payment would come from, but they decided they just couldn't loan to a nonprofit even if I personally guaranteed it. Of course, we were unable to take out a loan for more than the property was worth so that deal fell through. Tired, disgusted, and even hurt because I wanted this property so bad, I knew we had to let it go and start all over again.

Needing some alone time, I drove home, fixed myself a cocktail, jumped in the tub for a long, hot bath. I just prayed and asked God to help me because I was getting tired and wanted to stop this process. The deadline to spend this grant money was also fast approaching and all I could think was, who gets access to $175,000 and can't spend it? This was taking too much time, it was too hard, and it was distracting me from other work that I needed to get done. So, I had my pity party and emotionally detached from that property.

By the next morning I put my big girl panties back on and was ready to get back to the drawing board. I began the day with my usual prayer and started looking for another property. As I told Jerome about my pity party he said, "You know the perfect property would be those duplexes on Main Street."

To my surprise there were four duplexes – a total of eight apartments – right there on Main Street with an open lot that had future room for growth. I could not believe my eyes because these duplexes were right across the street from the day care that I prayed about just a year earlier.

I instantly felt like these duplexes were perfect for what we wanted for the TLP program. With eight two-bedroom apartments they were just the right size and the location was perfect right up the street from our SCH and administrative offices. It was also across the street from a day care –not House of Dawn's day care just yet but I'm claiming that it will be one day – and next door to the city's police station.

While I felt everything about these buildings was perfect, I had one problem . . . they weren't for sale. But I felt God telling me that this was the property – that's why he couldn't let the other deals go through because he had something better for us.

So, I didn't let their unavailability stop me. I knocked on doors in the complex only to find out that the owner didn't live on site and no one there would give me his contact information. So, I went into prayer and said if this was the property for us, please order my steps and order my words; make all the crooked paths straight and to go before me.

My next step was to look up the tax records to see who owned the property, then try to reach them and ask if they were willing to sell. I figured all they could say is no . . . you have not because you ask not, so I figured it was time to ask.

Finally, after searching through the tax records I found the name Robin Levi, but no telephone number. I called Mark, my real estate agent, to tell him how I wanted to make an offer to the guy who owned the property that wasn't for sale. Once I gave him the name, imagine my surprise to discover Mark had gone to school with someone who had the last name Levi – and he was sure they were related.

As he checked around, he found out that he went to school with Mr. Levi's daughter who still lived in the city limits. He was able to get her phone number, which in turn got us Mr. Levi's phone number.

As always, I prayed before making the call, and when Mr. Levi answered I got right to it.

"Mr. Levi, you don't know me, but my name is Dawn Murray and I'm interested in your property on South Main Street. I was wondering if you would be willing to meet with me to discuss?" Mr. Levi said that he lived in Lithonia but would be available to come down on Saturday afternoon and meet me at the property.

That Saturday a group of us had a brief meeting on the street in front of the duplexes with Mr. Levi. I asked would he be willing to sell the property and explained my plans for it.

"Well, I guess I'm willing to sell. I'm ninety-seven years old and will be dying soon. If I sell now my daughters won't have to worry about it once I'm gone. It won't be no negotiation I'll sell for $400,000 and throw in the extra land," he said.

Well just based on the tax records and the research we had already done, we knew that the land would appraise for more than that and from the looks of it, we would be going in with equity. I excitedly called the board members asking them to come take a look at the property and everyone was in favor.

Now the problem would be getting a loan in House of Dawn's name.

I went through a couple of companies and finally one said they would do it and let me personally guarantee it. But just as we were about to close – which took nearly eight months – we were told that the loan company would only do it in my name, not House of Dawn. On top of that, Mr. Levi would often remind me that he was dying soon and if the deal didn't go through, he would have to call everything off.

It was strange how Mr. Levi kept talking about dying because he seemed to be doing very well. He seemed to have all his wits about him. So, I took a chance and asked him and his daughter to come down for another meeting. I really had to pray, asking God for the courage to ask this question.

At our meeting, I sadly told Mr. Levi that the bank pulled out and will not loan to a nonprofit, but was willing to loan to me personally. The only catch is the property had to be in the House of Dawn's name. So I asked if there was any way he'd be willing to do owner financing.

I was really shaking in my boots, worried that he was going to rescind the offer. But surprisingly he said yes – with conditions.

He would receive an interest rate of 8 percent and it had to be refinanced within three years or else the property would revert back to him. While I didn't like these terms, I felt we had no other choice. I had already been given an extension on spending this $175,000 grant, and the deadline was looming. I knew this was the perfect property for the TLP, I just had to hustle and do one of two things: have it refinanced within three years (which I was told is much easier versus a new commercial loan); or have it paid off in three years which meant writing grants, and fundraising like hell. I wasn't afraid of hard work and knew I could do one of these, so I agreed to his terms. Mark started moving things forward and within thirty days we went to closing on the multi-dwelling with Mr. Levi doing owner financing for us.

Mr. Levi lived seven more months after we closed. He was truly getting all of his affairs in order and ended up selling more of his properties during this time. I guess he was right and knew he would be transitioning from this life.

Chapter 15

BIRTH OF NONPROFIT SUCCESS

As House of Dawn continued growing and becoming a success I was spending less time advising people how to start their own nonprofits. At this point in my career, I had consulted so many people and nonprofits on ways to open their businesses that I truly lost count.

Checklist 8: Instructions on How to Start a Residential Program.

Ms. Kerwin, who was House of Dawn's director at the time, said, "You can't keep meeting with people individually and you can't keep doing this for free. You just don't have the time anymore." I made a decision then that I only needed to deal with serious people who were ready to commit.

But I knew that she was right about meeting with everyone individually. That's when Ms. Kerwin suggested that I offer one workshop to show people how to start a nonprofit.

That day, my "Nonprofit Success" business was born – a for-profit project that helped nonprofits succeed. My goal was to help people with likeminded passions who in turn want to help others start their own organizations the right way. I wanted to help others build a foundation, start it as a business, and continue treating it as a business to ensure sustainability. I shared everything that I knew, but it was most important for me to see that they were willing to invest in themselves and their businesses.

I set up my first workshop, scheduled for a half-day. I had about twenty attendees out the gate and for $79, I provided breakfast along with a wealth of information.

That was three years ago and since then Nonprofit Success has grown into a series of workshops that takes you on a journey from the beginning of starting a nonprofit to actually opening and operating a residential program. The course also includes a coaching program that comes with examples of everything so that you don't have to reinvent the wheel while providing the tools to develop your own program.

Remember, I told God that when he blessed me with House of Dawn I would help as many people as possible. It doesn't get any easier than what my step-by-step instructions offer, but this journey is a lot of work – and you must be willing to put in the work. I don't start the program for you but I will impart all of my knowledge. And if you stay the course, the outcome will be so worth it!

Chapter 16
YOU HAVE TO MOVE -
SECOND CHANCE HAS BEEN
SOLD

One December afternoon in 2017, Taneisha and I were working in our office when the phone rang. The caller ID told me it was our SCH landlord and while staring at the ringing phone I immediately felt uneasy.

"I'm not answering it," I told Taneisha. It's our landlord and for some reason, I don't think it's good news. I think he sold the house."

"What?" Taneisha replied. "Why do you think that?"

I didn't know why; it was just a feeling. I told Taneisha I wasn't ready to hear what he had to say yet.

I waited about an hour before calling him back. "Dawn, we sold the property to a developer, and we closed today. The new landlord will be reaching out to you. I'm not sure if you will have sixty or ninety days to vacate the premises, but that will be up to him. Thank you for being a good tenant," said the voice on the other end of the phone. My instincts were correct.

The first thing that I thought about was Mrs. Smith, whom I originally rented the house from. She wouldn't have handled it this way; she would have made sure that we were okay. This was the hand House of Dawn was dealt, but I knew God had us and would take care of everything. I wasn't nervous. I didn't have any fear. I just trusted God.

I initially kept the news to myself so as not to make anyone nervous. I did eventually tell the administrative staff, director, and case management team what we were facing, and assured them we had nothing to worry about. I believe because I wasn't showing fear they felt confident that everything would be okay.

I received a call from a local businessman. He and his sister wanted to meet, but I was on my way out of town for the holiday. I figured maybe they wanted to look at partnering with House of Dawn in the new year, so I was eager to meet with them upon my return.

They stopped by House of Dawn in early 2018, and I personally gave them the full tour, explaining our program and how much we had grown since we first started.

During our tour, I could see the surprised look on their faces at how many people we had working in that small office and how cramped we were.

Once we sat down and started talking, to my surprise, I found out that they were actually the new owners of the property. This meeting was to discuss them being our landlords and to let us know that House of Dawn was not going to be put out of our SCH, that we could take our time finding another location.

I shared my vision that the goal of the TLP program was to eventually build a SCH on that lot. I guess it was time to move forward with that vision, but it would take some time because we had to secure funding as well. They were very understanding and told me not to lose any sleep about having to moving out of the SCH home before we were ready.

My prayers had been answered! But now I just had to work on the biggest part – how would we get the money to make all of this happen? I knew that God wasn't finished and also believed that he didn't intend for us to have a mortgage on this new home.

If God gave you the vision, HE will make the provisions!

A few weeks later they had another surprise. Renovations were being completed on Mrs. Smith's old home, and they offered to let us move our office into this much bigger home at the same price House of Dawn was already paying in rent. My mouth dropped! We were finally getting the bigger space that we so desperately needed.

What was even more exciting is that this was the home of one of House of Dawn's first supporters and my first champion who fought to have our program in this community. It was an honor to have House of Dawn's administrative offices located in Mrs. Smith's home. That warmed my heart more than anything.

Once the work was complete, they took me on a personal tour of the renovated home. At one point, they directed me to a room with a private entrance. "As the CEO of this agency you deserve your own office," the businessman announced.

For the first time since House of Dawn opened its doors, I had my own office! And I could not wait to make it look like the CEO's office I had always dreamed about.

Blessings were raining down on House of Dawn, but I couldn't get caught up in it all because I still had to find funding to purchase a new SCH. So, I started looking for funders that focused on building campaigns.

The CDBG discovered that a local funder, the Clayton County Housing Authority, was looking to donate up to $30,000 to reliable agencies working hard in the community. They told them about House of Dawn, so I contacted the funder and set up a meeting to give him more information about our program and a tour of the agency.

When the Clayton County Housing Authority representative came out, he seemed impressed with what we were doing for homeless young mothers and their children. I was then invited to speak at their next board meeting. Of course, I agreed, sensing this could be big for House of Dawn. I spent the next weeks preparing and could not wait to do a presentation for them.

Then the unthinkable happened the morning of the presentation. As I tried to get out of bed, I couldn't stand up straight. My back was out and despite using rubs, taking pain relievers, wearing a back brace, and laying on a heating pad, I was still in extreme pain. I knew that if I didn't make it to this board meeting, I'd have to wait until the following month for another chance to present. The funds could be distributed elsewhere by then – I was determined to do this presentation if I had to crawl in there.

I eased into the car with all of House of Dawn's materials and drove to the Clayton County Housing Authority's office. Instead of going inside right away, I waited until it was closer to presentation time. I was still in pain but straightened up enough to appear okay.

Throughout my presentation, I could tell by their reactions, head nods, and smiles that the board members liked what I had to say. They enjoyed the House of Dawn video and seeing the work that we were doing in the community, which felt good. I then opened the floor up for questions, and they seemed delighted and satisfied with my answers, until I was asked:

"What is it that your agency needs the most?"

I knew the answer, but suddenly felt afraid to say it aloud as a big lump formed in my throat and the room got very hot. I was embarrassed by my hesitation after everything seemed to be going so well.

All of the sudden I heard the Lord say, *"You have not because you ask not, I didn't give you the spirit of fear!"* And in that moment, I got my self-confidence back.

"What we need most is a new SCH for our teen moms and babies to live. We have the land, but we need a home built on it, we were just informed that the home that we have been residing in for the last 14 years has been sold." I answered.

That's when the questions really started flying. "How much do you think it will cost to build your home?" one gentleman asked. I got another lump in my throat and when the words finally came out, I was just beating around the bush.

"Are you not sure of the cost?" he inquired, cutting my rambling off.

I was afraid to say the number out loud because I knew that the Clayton County Housing Authority was only offering up to $30,000 – a number that I was very comfortable asking for.

"It will cost about $350,000 to build this home. We are now in the process of finalizing the drawings and having it designed, but we have set a $350,000 budget," I acknowledged.

I write (and have been awarded) grants for large sums all the time, but until now I was not yet comfortable asking for such a large amount of money in person. Post-presentation, I felt very good about it.

I packed up my items, thanked everyone for their time, and walked back to my car. I only hoped I was playing it off and that no one could tell just how much I was still hurting. I made it back home to my heating pad, opened my prayer journal, and talked to God about my experience. I thanked Him for giving me the strength to make it to the meeting and the courage to honestly answer all of their questions.

The next day I had less pain, but was able to move around better and drive. Ironically, my sister was having back surgery so I went to the hospital to see her. While there I received a call from the Clayton County Housing Authority's director, so I stepped into the hall.

He told me that they were impressed with my presentation and all of the wonderful work that we were doing. This is why they looked forward to assisting House of Dawn with funding. He then listed the possibilities: (1) they could write House of Dawn a check for operations for $25,000 to $30,000, or (2) they could assist us with building our SCH, they would own the building and we could lease it from them for a $1 per month. However the offer of building assistance came with concerns of what happens to House of Dawn if something happens to me. I then explained the succession plan our board had in place, and the director asked me to email a copy to share and discuss with the other members.

Look at God! He was now answering the other part of the prayer that there be no mortgage on this SCH. He knew we needed a new home which we couldn't afford to buy, didn't have a down payment for, and the vision was to stop paying high dollar rent, allowing us to use that money to instead operate the program.

If God gave you the vision, HE will make the provisions!

Chapter 17

HOUSE OF DAWN EXPANDS ITS VISION

God knew the plans He had for me. I pushed through the struggles and birthing pains of starting this nonprofit. I prevailed in laying claim when I had no money. I secured money for start-up costs with no options in sight. I persisted in getting licensed despite multiple rejections. I studied, researched, and taught myself as much as I could to find out what I needed to know to continue my journey. I also learned to develop programs, write policies and procedures, and grants.

I started a program with just a vision and eventually realized that even with trials, I could replicate those programs. This chapter looks at three programs that have helped expand this vision.

TRANSITIONAL LIVING PROGRAM

Our first group of young mothers were special for various reasons. Most of our moms were earning their GEDs, doing well with their parenting and life skills, and taking good care of their babies. But one mom named Latoya – who had become the leader that girls looked up to – started regressing when she had trouble passing her GED test. After taking the test twice she was only a few points off on one of her sections, so we just knew that the next time she would pass it. Most importantly, we wanted Latoya to receive her GED before she aged out of the program.

It soon became obvious that she was depressed; she wouldn't do anything, refused to take the GED test again, and wouldn't tell us what was wrong.

Eventually one of our more vocal girls, Shelly, spoke truth to power. "Y'all are excited because we're meeting the goals that you gave us, and that we'll be soon be old enough to complete this program. But that doesn't do us any good because, then what? Where do we go after we complete the program? House of Dawn is all that we have. We can't make it on our own out there . . . and if we don't make enough money to support our kids, they will stay in the custody of DFCS once we age out."

Well damn . . . I was crushed at that notion. Here we were all in our feelings, thinking it was a good thing that they were the first group to complete the program.

We needed another program that would go beyond age nineteen. We also needed an outlet for the moms to get our help if they hit hard times after leaving the program. It was important for them to know that when they progressed far enough to go out in the real world, we could still be there for them.

I immediately started looking for funding that would allow us to add an extension to the SCH. I started writing grants for a TLP to serve moms aged 18-21. I knew this would become a vital component to the long-term success of our families.

G-CAPP was one of the organizations that I submitted a proposal to, as they had applied for a larger TLP grant. Once they were awarded that grant they named House of Dawn as a sub-recipient, which allowed us to do a five-year pilot program for Transitional Living! Look at God!

Getting this funding would allow us to see if the program could work well, and we could still find more funding before the five-year pilot ended. This worked perfectly, as we miraculously got three funders to continue supporting the program. We also had enough funds to expand the program, doubling the capacity.

This funding allowed me to partner with an apartment complex where House of Dawn rented one-bedroom apartments (before we started purchasing our own properties). We received plenty of furniture donations and G-CAPP also had funds worked into our grant to purchase items that didn't get donated.

On May 15, 2007, exactly two years after we opened our SCH, the TLP program moved in. While I was sad that we didn't have the program open in enough time to help Latoya, we vowed to do our best so as not to lose another young mother in this way. House of Dawn now provides a bridge to help these moms get to the next level.

*   *   *

INDEPENDENT LIVING PROGRAM

After extending the program so our moms could transition from SCH to TLP, we also noticed that our 18- to 21-year-olds were just not developmentally ready to live completely on their own without supervision from the agency Life Coach. They would constantly sneak guys over and allow unstable parents and family members to stay with them – some of whom were homeless themselves.

So, I started thinking: wouldn't it be great to have our young moms (ages 13-18) with 24-hour supervision; our middle-aged moms (ages 18-21) with evening and overnight supervision; and our older moms (ages 21-24) with only a 24-7 on call life coach for emergencies. To do this, we extended our service range to age 24 because we constantly received calls from young mothers in need between the ages of 21 and 24. This allowed us to implement these important changes so that those who have gone through the program could mentor their peers and experience graduated independence.

House of Dawn remains the only program in this community serving pregnant and parenting homeless youth. In the past, there were no homeless resources available to them and nowhere for them to go. Other homeless shelters in the community served people starting at age 25, and they couldn't be pregnant. Accordingly, House of Dawn decided to extend the service age to 24 to bridge that gap in order to serve these mothers too – which is when the Independent Living Program (ILP) was born!

Despite the undeniable need, we did not have the means to rent any more facilities. And we didn't have funding to support this program. Again, I prayed and asked God to bless us with the provisions to start this much needed initiative.

Incidentally, I found out Chase Bank had a program that donated foreclosed homes to nonprofits. I did my research and immediately started the application process. I was eventually approved and granted access to look at foreclosed properties that they had available. I was so excited to find one in Riverdale, which was only ten minutes from our TLP program.

Some of the board members and I toured it, and we couldn't believe our eyes! I initially thought there was no way we would ever be able to bring this home up to code – all of the copper had been removed and the heating and air conditioning units were long gone. The house had enormous holes in the walls and ceilings. Squirrels had eaten through the wood on the outside. And to top that off, a squatter was still living in it!

I accepted the donation not knowing what we could do with it. Jerome said it was a mess, but we could just take our time and rebuild it. He and our then-board chair immediately went to work on the house. They gutted the inside so that we could see what we genuinely had to work with. They felt the home had potential, so the work began on the space for the ILP program. My kids thought the house was so ugly that they dubbed it "The Cabin" and the name stuck!

We received many donations for this reclaimed home. As the remodeling project continued, I searched for funding to restore and operate the Cabin.

This home had truly become a labor of love for our board of directors. A lot of sweat equity went into this project until we were finally able to renovate the inside. We did our "Adopt a Room" program again, allowing local groups such as the Rotary Club of Clayton County, the Clayton County Grassroots Leadership Institute, and others to decorate the home. They all helped to create a beautiful living space for our moms and their new arrivals.

The donated house was lovely but the squirrels literally continued to be a gnawing problem. They would eat through the wood on the outside of the house and gain access to the attic as well as the roof and behind the walls. As quickly as the holes would get patched up, the squirrels seemed to chew through the wood even faster. Even squirrel traps could not discourage them for long. We knew the only way to solve this problem was to affix a new roof and aluminum siding. This would be a costly expense that more than likely we would be unable to secure donations for. I tried writing grants for this also, but received no awards up until this point.

In the meantime, I knew from experience that it would take some time to get licensing, zoning, and funding. But the funding would come and the squirrels would go; it was just a matter of time.

Eventually, we were awarded $15,000 through a CDBG grant that would allow us to finish the remaining needed renovations. We finally added a roof and aluminum siding and after the work was completed, we went from having the worst looking home on the block to the best! And most importantly, we didn't have to battle squirrels anymore.

*   *   *

HOUSE OF DAWN GOES GLOBAL

While this is a longways off, my goal is to one day retire, sit on the board, and ensure that the House of Dawn legacy continues. So, when my daughter Bria expressed an interest in working with House of Dawn, I let her know that if it's what she really wanted and she worked hard, I would be honored for her to continue House of Dawn in my stead. But the opportunity to lead must be earned just as with any other employee.

"Mommy when I move up in House of Dawn one day, I want us to go global!" Bria said. "I want to take it to another level. I want to serve moms and babies in other countries that are in need."

I knew that we wouldn't have to wait that long. My dear friend Andrea prophesied about four years earlier that God told her House of Dawn was supposed to go global because we were needed in Ghana, Africa. We didn't have the funds for that type of mission work yet, but Bria's words were confirmation that I needed to start working on the House of Dawn's global outreach right now.

I told her to get a clean notebook, label it "House of Dawn Goes Global", and start writing her vision. "Write down who you want to serve, what services you want to bring them, and what you want to do while you're there," I advised.

I called a couple of my board members that had worked on mission trips to see what all was involved. They were excited about the possibilities and suggested Jamaica because some of them had already done missions there and had connections. The country also happened to be Bria's favorite travel destination (so far), so it seemed perfect. And with that, the first "House of Dawn Goes Global" Committee was founded with five people.

Bria designed a House of Dawn drawstring bag that would hold personal hygiene items for fifty moms which included reusable maxi pads, and disposable nursing pads, maxi pads, condoms, soap, deodorant, and personal hygiene wipes.

For the babies, we collected disposable diapers, blankets, crib sheets, baby bottles, and onesies, and their bags were donated by Atlanta's Emory Hospital. Our House of Dawn moms used puff paint to decorate the onesies with "House of Dawn" and other personal notes of encouragement.

We held a fundraiser that despite its low turnout collected $1,500, which was enough to purchase the rest of the items needed to fill the bags and cover the expenses incurred for shipping the items to Jamaica. We even received a donated trunk full of brand-new sneakers, so we were able to bless about twenty boys and girls with new shoes.

Our day of mission work finally, and we were able to complete our mission right on the streets of Clairmont, Jamaica. We distributed personal hygiene supplies for mom and babies, baby clothes, and Christmas hats and toys to the children.

So many people were involved in helping to spread this vision of education, self-reliance, and encouragement overseas. While we are unsure where God will have us travel to do his work next, we do know that our House of Dawn Global Committee is already planning its next mission!

Chapter 18

OUR NEW SECOND CHANCE HOME

Over the last fifteen years of operation, the city and House of Dawn had built a great working relationship. I am happy to say that our program is fully supported and welcomed in the city and community.

Now that the Clayton County Housing Authority had agreed to finance House of Dawn's new SCH, we needed to figure out the steps to building a new home. While this was a major step forward there was so much work that had to go into this project, starting with creating architectural drawings of the home.

Setting a zoning date with the city was the next order of business, a task which did get easier the second time around. The problem was I didn't realize our TLP was located on land in a historical district, and that comes with stricter requirements. This meant we had to hire an attorney to ensure a successful outcome. Thankfully our then-board chair was able to retain Hecht Walker PC pro bono. This was yet another major expense House of Dawn did not incur.

In March 2018 the City Council placed zoning signs in the yard for thirty days to alert the community of our request. However, a few weeks before the zoning meeting

I asked if we could be taken off the calendar because our architectural drawings were incomplete and I didn't want to go in unprepared. Mandy, House of Dawn's building project manager for HomeAid Atlanta, found some Georgia Tech students willing to take this on as a class project, saving us financially yet again.

We started with a tour of the SCH home, where I explained the changes that needed to be included in the new home. The young moms currently living in the SCH also shared their input about additions to the home's design. Within a few weeks the drawings were complete and we were ready to go before City Council. Thanks to those Georgia Tech students and Hecht Walker's legal expertise, House of Dawn passed zoning with the city to build our new SCH.

This was definitely a day to remember and the start of another chapter for House of Dawn.

Checklist 9: How to Prepare for Building a Structure. Below is a checklist of things we did to prepare for the building of our new facility.

☐ Develop a Budget

☐ Find Funding

☐ Design Your Facility (what spaces do you need to successfully execute your organization's plan?)

☐ Develop Architectural Drawings

☐ Select a Contractor

☐ Secure Builders Risk Insurance

☐ Engineered Drawing

☐ Apply for Zoning

☐ Apply for Land Disturbance Permit

☐ Apply for Building Permits

☐ Groundbreaking

☐ Start Building Your Facility!

Nonprofit Nugget: *Check with your local governmental entities to ensure you're following all of the steps to building a facility in your area.*

Chapter 19

THE DAWN OF A NEW DAY: LESSONS LEARNED DURING THIS TWENTY-YEAR JOURNEY

The journey I have chosen to take has blessed me to have countless positive people in my life that provide support and encouragement for me. The lessons I have learned are invaluable. However, if I had to select one very important lesson from this journey that I've taken, I would say it's learning to give myself self-love and self-care.

Another important lesson this journey has taught me is, everybody won't go with you. I'm glad to say that I've finally reached the point where I'm okay with that fact. As you find yourself moving to new levels – which undoubtedly means taking on new journeys – you will lose some people along the way that no longer share the same views and visions that you do. You need to prepare and accept that this will happen. Adjust yourself to discovering and embracing the people in your circle who will support you and are genuinely happy to see your growth and development.

As working women, mothers, wives, business owners, caregivers – and all of the roles we play for so many – we take care of everyone else and put ourselves last. I want women to know that we don't have to be Superwoman. It's okay to ask for help. It's okay to love on ourselves, and we shouldn't feel guilty about it. It's okay to say NO when you need to. And it's definitely okay not to overextend ourselves.

My journey for peace started about four years ago at a doctor's appointment. The doctor could see how stressed I was and she gave me a stress test – the first one I had ever taken. Returning for my follow-up appointment, she came in the room all excited, asking, "So, when are we going to do it? When is it going to be? We might as well plan for it at the rate you are going!"

Having no idea what she was talking about, I was taken aback, replying, "Plan for what? What are you talking about?"

"Your stroke," she answered in a very low and serious tone. "You are so stressed out you aren't even registering; your lines have gone beyond our stress chart. Whatever is going on with you, you have to make some changes in your life. If you don't, just plan your stoke because you are going to have one. It's just a matter of when."

A light bulb went off and I became very serious about the things that were going on in my life and major, nonnegotiable changes that I had to make. The realization that only I could change me put everything into perceptive. I started putting me first and doing things to promote my happiness and well-being.

I had to stop taking on the problems of others, trying to fix everyone and everybody, I had to do some serious soul searching and praying for my peace. At all costs, I was determined to give myself peace.

For numerous years I put everyone above my own feelings, and it has taken me forty-five years to be okay with saying no. I now know what's acceptable for me and what's not. It's taken me this long to put myself first and truly exercise self-love and self-care.

I was out one night having dinner with a colleague just catching up laughing and talking about our busy lives, when I explained to her that I was ready to live my life and "do me" for a change. "I'm sorry, I'm just feeling a little selfish these days and I need to take care of me," I confessed.

She suddenly stopped smiling and gave me a very stern look. "I better not ever hear you say that again! It's called self-love not selfishness and ain't a damn thing wrong with it! You do too much and for so many – you better not ever apologize for exercising self-love!"

The blessing of having positive, supportive, encouraging people in my life is their understanding of the value of putting me first. I was so used to coming in last . . . thinking about everyone else's needs and what was going to please them or make them happy that I would automatically say yes to doing things that I didn't really want to do. This is who I was and had been for so long.

My children Jam and Bria, were always supportive and would often remind me to put myself first sometimes. One evening Jam and I were in the kitchen talking and I told him I was thinking about getting rid of "Big Girl" (nickname for my Nissan Armada.) I had been driving a full-size SUV or mini-van for so many years because I had a big family. After Bria left for college, I started thinking I don't need this big truck with three rows any longer it's just me! I was ready to go back to driving a car and the one that I've wanted and had named, Noire, since I was fourteen years old. But when I'd start seriously considering a switch, I'd automatically say to myself, no I better keep Big Girl. I'll need the extra space when I have the grandkids with me.

Jam stopped, looked at me like I had three heads, and said "Ma, you have raised your kids! Now it's your turn to do what you want to do, drive what you want to drive, travel and go where you want to go! It's your turn! Stop thinking about everyone else! If you want the grandkids, tell their parents to drop them off. Go trade in your truck and get what you want."

Two days later I traded in Big Girl for Noire and drove her home. While driving I thought to myself, I like doing me! This feels good and this I must continue!

*   *   *

I've always enjoyed entertaining and having holidays at my home but I decided that I didn't want to do that anymore. For the first time in my life I now truly wanted to relax on the holidays. My seven-year-old grandson even told me that "Holidays are for relaxing, Nae-Nae."

I've talked about how nice it would be to have Christmas on the beach for years but never stopped having holidays at my home. I enjoyed it and everyone had a wonderful time but throwing big Christmas parties for the last twenty years had become tiring. Now that my children are grown, I am at a new place in my life of putting me first and doing what I want to do.

I remember telling my daughter, "Little Girl, I know I've been saying this for a few years now but I'm really thinking about canceling Christmas and going somewhere to relax. But our family and friends aren't used to that – everyone is used to coming here for Christmas Eve. Bria looked at me and said "Mommie, what do you want to do? You have to stop thinking about everyone else. If you want to go away for the holidays this year and relax, then do it! You've given your family and friends wonderful Christmas parties and now it's your turn to do what you want to do and how you want to do it."

So, for the first time I woke up on Christmas morning in 2018 to the beautiful sun rising on the beach, hearing the waves of the ocean crash along the shore while sipping coffee on my balcony. I couldn't have been happier! I was having Christmas on the beach surrounded by people that loved me and enjoyed seeing me happy and at peace.

You have to keep people in your circle that support you and that are truly happy to see your growth and your changes. One day one of my dear friends and I were chatting, and I shared how I'm where I want to be in life, living my best life, putting myself first, speaking and releasing anything that is heavy on my heart instead of walking around with all that extra weight and baggage. I'm no longer walking around holding things in to keep the peace or make everyone else happy I'm making myself happy and in search of my own peace. She was so excited to see this transformation, but did say, "Stay ready, because everyone won't understand your newfound happiness and it's only because they aren't used to it. You need to put yourself first, so be prepared for that, but keep that smile on your face and live life to the fullest – you only have one life to live and you better live!"

I've become so protective about my peace that I pray for it daily. My peace of mind and health are my priority and I have to release anything that chips away at my peace. I can't wait for someone to give it to me – it's my responsibility to ensure that my peace of mind is there and that it stays there. I'm at a point in my life where I don't do drama, nor do I even want to hear it. I just want to live a life of peace and relaxation and I'm proud that I've allowed myself to have it and enjoy it.

Your inner circle is so important! You need to have people that will uplift, encourage, and motivate. People that will speak life into you, your business, your family. A circle of support that will pray with you and for you, while also holding you accountable.

I've learned that you cannot continue to pour from an empty cup – you have to have people in your life that will replenish you so that you can continue to give to others and do the work that God has for you to do.

Yes, it is the Dawn of a New Day for me!

Epilogue
WELCOME TO NEW DAWN COURT!

During the final stages of this book I found out that the city approved the naming of our street that current and future House of Dawn properties will sit on. The land that will house our TLP and our new SCH have been zoned as a subdivision in the city and will now have its own street name: New Dawn Court.

We truly have come a very long way!

May 15, 2019 was also a day of celebrations for House of Dawn. We planned a ceremony with HomeAid Atlanta to do a ribbon cutting of our newly renovated TLP, adding new ADA compliant bathrooms to each of the units. But instead of a room, we executed "adopt a bathroom" which were decorated by the Clayton County Chamber of Commerce's Women in Business Committee, the Zeta Phi Beta sorority, Ollies Place for Specialty Suites, Divine Faith Ministries, and Global Impact Christian Ministries.

We also held a beautiful groundbreaking ceremony that was well attended by elected officials, community leaders, some of our funders, community partners – especially the builder, Knight Homes and HomeAid Atlanta – and so many that have been a part of this journey from the beginning.

*　　*　　*

From first working with teen mothers as a mentor through the Clayton County Cooperative Extension to becoming a Parenting Educator to working my way up to the CEO of House of Dawn, Inc., my vision and dream, is now a reality.

I have always wanted these young mothers to believe and recognize they can still be successful, they can still finish school, secure stable employment, and provide for their children despite the challenges and naysayers. Even more important, they have the opportunity to change the lives of their children.

It is also important that these young mothers recognize that neither they nor their children are destined to become a statistic. When they are exposed to another way of life, a circle of support surrounds them and the barriers of being a young mother are removed. When you know better, you can do better!

I have seen so many grow into adults who are educated, working, and homeowners. Some are married and some live independently – but all are loving mothers to their children who truly continue to live House of Dawn's mission! It warms my heart and often brings tears to my eyes.

House of Dawn has grown so much over the last fifteen years and I have so many people to thank for the growth and the sustainability of this organization. It has been an honor and a privilege to travel this journey which allowed me to help thousands of pregnant and parenting young mothers and their children.

I'm thankful for every struggle, which taught me how to start, own, and operate every aspect of my business. This invaluable experience allowed me to expand my organization up to five programs, and fifteen years later it has also given me a for-profit business as well called "Nonprofit Success." My success in building a nonprofit organization now puts me in a position to help others with a likeminded passion to start their own nonprofit.

I'm so glad that I kept listening to God and being obedient. I also know that He still has more work for me to do. I look forward to what He has in store for the House of Dawn organization and to see the promises and blessings that await the families that come through our doors.

ABOUT THE AUTHOR

Dawn L. Murray is the Founder/CEO of **House of Dawn, Inc**, a non-profit organization that provides a stable, loving home for teen mothers and their children. Dawn holds a BS in Human Services and in Business Administration from Shorter University. Dawn has several certifications and trainings in the area of nonprofit management, including, nonprofit finance & accounting essentials.

Dawn has worked her passion, helping pregnant and parenting teen mothers in various ways since 1999 in Clayton County Georgia. Working this path Dawn often encountered teen mothers in need of a safe haven for themselves as well as their children. Faced with this need for second chance housing, Dawn took her passion and twisted it to fit the need and created, a **Second Chance Home** in May of 2005. Second Chance Homes provides a safe space for teenage mothers ages 13-18 and their children. It also provides housing and family centric supportive services to pregnant and parenting youth.

While successfully operating House of Dawn, Inc, Dawn L. Murray has positioned herself to be a leader establishing herself as a motivation speaker, instructional trainer, author and business industry leader. She has also worked tirelessly establishing herself as a Non-Profit Strategist for her business **Non-Profit Success** a for profit business **helping nonprofits succeed**. Her skills and ability have paved the way for her to successfully give guidance and help to other nonprofits, leading them down a path to success.

As the owner of **Nonprofit Success**, Dawn has been sharing her passion, experience and, business success in taking nonprofits from start-up to sustainability by facilitating workshops, trainings, and a nonprofit coaching program. Utilizing her 20 years of experience as a successful nonprofit endeavor Dawn has raised over 10 million dollars in funding for the **House of Dawn** and has helped thousands of families in their quest to better themselves and their lives. The success that Dawn has achieved is undeniable.

Dawn has now expanded **House of Dawn, Inc** into various programs and services that include:

Independent Living Program (ages 18-21)

Transitional Housing Program (ages 21-24)

Homeless Prevention Program

Global Outreach Program that provides services to mothers and children internationaly.

Dawn is also a member of the Clayton County Rotary Club, and the Women in Business Executive Committee for the Clayton County Chamber of Commerce. She lives in Atlanta, Georgia.